KEEP GROWING

How to encourage students to persevere, overcome setbacks, and develop a growth mindset

Joey Mandel

Pembroke Publishers Limited

© 2017 Pembroke Publishers
538 Hood Road
Markham, Ontario, Canada L3R 3K9
www.pembrokepublishers.com

Distributed in the U.S. by Stenhouse Publishers
P.O. Box 11020
Portland, ME 04104
www.stenhouse.com

Library and Archives Canada Cataloguing in Publication

Mandel, Joey, author
    Keep growing : how to encourage students to persevere, overcome setbacks, and develop a growth mindset / Joey Mandel.

Issued in print and electronic formats.
ISBN 978-1-55138-320-0 (softcover).--ISBN 978-1-55138-921-9 (PDF)

    1. Character--Study and teaching (Elementary)--Activity programs. I. Title.

LC268.M35 2016   370.11'4   C2016-907632-6
                                       C2016-907633-4

Editor: Kat Mototsune
Cover Design: John Zehethofer
Typesetting: Jay Tee Graphics Ltd.

Printed and bound in Canada
9 8 7 6 5 4 3 2 1

MIX
Paper from
responsible sources
FSC
www.fsc.org   FSC® C004071

Contents

Introduction

"If I fall down, then I can get back up."

"If I miss a shot, then I should practice more often."

"If I do not know what to do, then I can figure it out."

In respect and support for trans-gendered students, the pronoun *they* will be used to refer to all individuals.

As I write these words, I have a clear image of certain children in my head, children for whom this kind of self-talk seems to come easily and naturally. These students are intrigued by the unknown. They want to get my feedback and then make changes to reflect it. They get excited by challenges. These children are easy to teach. It does not matter if they struggle or are strong academically, because for them the process of being shown what they need to work on, having it explained to them, and then practicing it is seamless. They are easy to teach because they are on board with the teaching plan in place, so the energy of the teacher goes toward teaching the material, not negotiating the task.

But then there is the other self-talk, the negative kind.

"This is too hard for me."

"It does not work."

"The teacher told me that I needed to change part of my project. She is always so mean to me."

"Why should I bother trying when I can't change anything anyway?"

"I can't do it."

"I will never be able to."

"My work will never be good enough."

These are all ways of thinking that can stop a child in their tracks, freeze their brains, and shut them down. What happens then? The student might stop participating in class or engage in distracting or disruptive behavior.

Students' willingness or ability to complete non-preferred tasks is easy to see during class transitions. Class transitions occur many times a day as we move from one activity to the next. It is a class job that is not really enjoyable or fun, yet it is necessary to the functioning of the classroom. As we finish one lesson and shift toward another, objects in the room need to be put away and new materials need to be set up. As teacher, I can co-create detailed lists, charts, and rubrics of what it looks like to help set up the room; I can motivate the students to get on board as valuable contributing members of their classroom; I can give proactive explanations that detail exactly what we will do, why we will do it, and the consequences for not doing it; finally, and most importantly, I can ask my students who will help. They all put their hands up but, as the process of setting up begins, their behaviors do not match the verbal commitments they make.

Any teacher can predict the response of each student to a request to do a non-preferred task or job. There would be students who immediately do what the teacher asked; they would do the jobs well and might even do more than what was asked. There would be students who stand there, unsure of what to do until the teacher approached them individually, pointed to the list of what needed to be done, and encouraged them to begin the first step. There would be students who rush to the teacher and check in to make sure that they knew what they were doing, ensure that they were doing it right, and tell the teacher once they were done. Finally, there would be students who do not even start the task. These students go off and chat or do something that they wanted, just outside the view of the teacher.

Is this it? Are these patterns of behavior established in early childhood? Are they therefore irreversible? Current research on the plasticity of the brain allows us to be hopeful that the writing is not on the wall. The future is not set. Predispositions in academic and social intelligence are malleable. Studies reveal that there are influencing factors that predispose children to be more willing to do hard things, to try something new, and to work hard to learn something that they were not able to learn the day before; further, these studies pinpoint what it is that influences children. We can look at these studies in order to gain insight into the way children mentally approach a task and the way strategies move them through hard tasks. And we can use that information in our teaching

A key concept to consider is the growth mindset. "Mistakes mean that I am trying" and "I can learn from my mistakes" are self-statements that exemplify growth mindset thinking. Every minute in the classroom we see examples of students making mistakes. Some students can then make quick choices that signal an openness to growth. We can capitalize on these choices, encouraging them to take ownership of their behavior without guilt or shame, to use what they learn, to apply it and make better choices next time. Growth mindset leads to the development of personality traits that show self-control.

How do we bring these principles directly into the classroom to assist students, day in and day out? How do we, as teachers, provide opportunities for children to change their mindsets? How do we foster and nurture their ability and desire to start hard tasks and push through them when they are stuck, to try something new when they do not know the answer, to build a sense of value for the effort and the completion of an activity over the success of it, and, finally, to work on or add to something that they have finished in order to make it better?

Drawing upon research that highlights the importance of self-control and growth mindsets, this book moves theory into teachable moments. It focuses on curriculum subjects that are already part of the classroom teaching practice and provides examples on applying them to aspects of growth mindset and self-control. It suggests usable classroom strategies, offers student activities, and provides assessment tools that are explicitly aimed to develop stronger student mindsets and increase problem-solving abilities. With direct examples, the book shows teachers how to assist students to become more aware of their thinking and to develop positive self-talk through *If/Then* scenarios. This will help students to set goals, problem-solve, and face challenges in a more self-directed way.

Sometimes, as teachers, we wonder what home life looks like for these last children. What are they allowed to get away with there? But years of teaching (and having children of my own) have proven to me that these behaviors cannot be explained by over-indulgent parents who do not expect anything from their children. Families with multiple children might have one child who immediately helps at home and follows expectations without needing anything in return, while another child needs consistent reminders and prompts to do each step of a job, along with rewards for each action.

Grit, perseverance, resilience, and self-regulation are terms teachers and parents are hearing a lot lately. Children with these traits are said to be better able to cope with life's adversities and obstacles, to face challenges and recover from setbacks, and therefore to be more successful and happier individuals.

1

Mindset for Growth

"I am bored." "I don't want to do this." "Can I draw instead?" "What else can I do?"

When I prompt students that we are about to begin a task, be it a math lesson, guided reading, or a standardized test, some will always say, "I don't want to." To myself, I think about the twenty things that I have just done that I "don't want to"! It is clear that, in a sense, no one (including me) really wants to do that particular activity. But it is our next step, our next job in the day. It is on the set schedule of the day and it needs to be done. So, as a whole class, we begin that task, even though it is nobody's preferred activity. Most students recognize that this is the next step in the day; they begin the task and participate in this less-enjoyable-than-most school activity. Some students begin the interplay between student and teacher of prompts and resistance to each task; they eagerly look at the clock, awaiting recess, leaving the teacher to try to navigate the process of expectations, motivation, negotiations, and consequences. This draws out the activity and makes it miserable for all. As teachers, we are left wondering if some of our students should be allowed to go out for recess, when they have not worked to their abilities or tried their best.

If you don't think you can do something, if you think your work will never be good enough, it would be very difficult to want to try. It would be hard to begin a task that you think you could never accomplish properly.

Mindsets

Mindset is a concept introduced by Carol Dweck in *Mindset: The New Psychology of Success* (2006).

Mindsets are attitudes and dispositions that influence the way children view obstacles, challenges, and hard situations in life. A *fixed mindset* is the belief that IQ is predetermined and static. In fixed mindset, the end task or the result is what matters most. The product at the end is how the task will be judged. A good grade and positive feedback are the measures of success. (Dweck, 2006, p. 8)

On the other hand, a *growth mindset* is the belief that intelligence can grow with hard work and effort. People with growth mindsets understand the value in the process and the learning along the way. Low grades might be messages to work harder; feedback is interpreted as giving ways to improve.

Self-reflection on these questions could help you determine whether you have a Fixed or Growth Mindset.

- Would you rather see your team win a game against a weaker team, or see it lose to a more advanced team that challenged you?
- Would you rather get a poor mark on a test that you studied hard for and learned a lot of cool information for, or get a great mark on a test that was so easy you did not need to study?
- Would you rather stumble on a few words during your presentation as you present to the class, or get a pass and not have to present at all?
- Would you rather try something you have never tried before and do it wrong, or would you rather not try it at all?

As teachers, we can reflect on our own mindsets, examine them in nonjudgmental ways, and rethink them. If our mindsets shift and influence how we feel and behave, we can help our students through the same process.

The mindset you adopt, fixed or growth, affects the way you act and respond to daily challenges. It determines whether you walk away, give up, and complain, or you attempt to meet the challenge with a positive and optimistic attitude. A child's willingness to confront challenges and see them through could be linked to the way they have come to think and feel about success. Children who believe that they need to succeed feel pressure to perform well and be perfect and to complete tasks in an exceptional way. These children struggle much more to begin tasks, to continue them when they are hard, and to complete them. The pressure these children put on themselves to achieve success, perfection, and accomplishment affects their ability to take the steps needed to try. They can become overcome by worrying whether they will do it correctly, how to do it, and if it will be done well. On the other hand, children who see success as just trying or learning something new are able to approach tasks with less pressure and more excitement, as it is the process of learning that is the mark of success, not the product of the task. This second group of children have growth mindsets.

Growth mindset is reflected in optimistic thinking and positive self-talk: thinking that says "Cool, I love a challenge," or "This looks tricky; it could be fun," "It is important to try," or "If I work at it hard enough, I might figure something out." This kind of self-talk leads to the development of effective learning strategies: "If it is hard, I should try a few different approaches before asking for help." "I was able to do something similar to this problem before, so if I work at this, I will likely be able to figure it out too."

Imagine if we all approached challenges with this self-talk. There is determination in this kind of thinking. Unknowns are not scary; missteps are not failures. There is a desire to do well and to succeed, but there is less stress on the need to do it perfectly. Pressure is removed when part of the value is in the attempt and the process itself.

This approach to work is based in a belief in oneself, in self-talk that says, "I can do it." This type of positive thinking opens responses instead of shutting them down. It focuses on the value of trying and the learning experience itself, rather than on the success or failure of the task at hand. This self-confidence helps individuals make tough choices and push through when the going gets hard, because the goal is not in doing something perfectly, but instead in doing something to the best of your ability. There is value in the way you get there and in trying to get there on your own.

Students have their own immediate thoughts about every problem or challenge. These quick thoughts are influenced by many things: their predisposition toward a way of thinking, their ability to perform a particular activity; their past experience in successfully overcoming challenges; and the support system around them. As we learn about each student's natural response to adversity, including the factors that influence that response, we can begin to help them build their own awareness of these responses. This can lead them to an understanding of their power and control over these responses.

Key Mindset Points

- People think differently when they are faced with challenges.
- It is important to be willing and able to reflect upon how you think about challenges, obstacles, or setbacks.
- If you can change the way you think about challenges, obstacles, or setbacks, you can change the way you act when faced with them.

The Marshmallow Test and Self-Control

In 1960, Stanford professor Walter Mischel conducted experiments to try to determine a relationship between a child's willpower and IQ. What he found was that there was no link between a child's ability to delay gratification and their intellectual abilities; instead, he found that a child's ability to put off something they want immediately is strongly connected to that child's success in any area of life, including school. Children who were able to delay gratification using self-control skills tended to think ahead more often, plan more, pursue goals, and be more attentive. (Mischel, p. 26)

The Marshmallow Test

Researcher Walter Mischel told children they could have one marshmallow right away, or two marshmallows if they waited a certain amount of time. He recorded which children ate the marshmallow right away and which waited so that they could have two.

He observed the children while they waited and talked to them after the experiment, so that he knew what they were doing and thinking during the process. He saw the strategies they used to successfully delay getting something they wanted right away. He asked students to explain to him the tricks they used. Some invented imaginary games using their fingers; for example, they played the piano on the table. Others invented songs or sang songs they already knew. They told themselves stories in their head. Children looked away from the marshmallow or closed their eyes, so that they could not see what was tempting them. As well, children told themselves encouraging things: "You can do it" or "If you wait, you get two." It was clear that children had clear strategies to distract themselves from the reward or to motivate themselves to wait for it.

While the experiment showed no correlation between intelligence and the ability to delay gratification, it revealed a lot of interesting information about the advantages of self-control. As the test subjects grew up, the ones who waited for two marshmallows did better in school; they studied more; they did their homework more often. Socially, they struggled less, had fewer conflicts, got into fewer fights, and were less involved in drug use. The findings held true through adulthood: kids who waited for two marshmallows reached their long-term goals more often and typically went further in school. They were less likely to get divorced and reported they were more content with life. They were less involved in drug use, had higher education, had lower body mass, and maintained better relationships.

When Mischel asked students if they wanted to eat one marshmallow right away or if they wanted to wait and then have two, most children said they wanted to wait. So from the beginning, most children started out wanting the bigger reward and challenged themselves with the harder task. But as time went on, only some of the children were able to sustain the effort needed to achieve the goal. From this study, we find the following:

- The way we think about a task influences how we approach it.
- The tools and strategies we have and use to help us move through tasks affect our success.
- These tools and strategies can be explained, taught, and developed, in adults and children alike, in order to develop the self-control needed to face hard tasks.

Mischel proved the link between self-control and success; what he observed was that the delayers, those who waited for something better, had strategies to help them do that. They had tricks and techniques that made it possible for them to wait and not give in, to keep themselves from eating the marshmallow in front of them. The delayers created ways to distract themselves in order to pass the time and resist the temptation of the marshmallow. Mischel's study revealed that student success in facing challenges is in large part influenced by the strategies they use in order to meet obstacles and challenging moments. As teachers, we can use these strategies with our students. The children in the study who were successful had both the mindset to want to achieve the task and a strategy that helped them follow through. These children had self-talk strategies that emphasized *what* they wanted and *how* to get it: *If I want two marshmallows, then I need to wait; If I distract myself, I won't be as tempted by the one marshmallow.* These internal *If/Then* statements allowed the children, on their own, to understand what they wanted and how to get it.

Approaching Life with *If/Then* Strategies

Life is full of unknowns and setbacks, yet some people do not run away from them. They approach challenges with caution, preparedness, and ideas; they are ready to try things and do non-preferred tasks. They possess something that allows them to begin and do things that are not easy or fun, as they have an understanding of the value of different rewards and success. Their heads are full of self-talk that says, "I can do this," or "I wonder how I should try to do this." These children stay with the task, even if it is hard, and they sit through the lesson, even when they are bored or confused. They show self-control.

Some children freeze when faced with a task that is unpleasant, difficult, or unknown. They look to others in desperation, hoping someone will tell them what to do, tell them they do not have to do it, or do it for them. They are caught

Wanting to know at what age he might witness self-control, Walter Mischel studied younger and younger children. He observed that the roots of self-control are visible in toddlers.

by self-talk that says, "I can't do this," and "I don't know the right thing to do." Some children struggle with extreme emotion when they lose, are confused, have to do something they don't want to do, or have to wait. Without support, they react in unproductive ways to life's adversities. They run away, give up, or engage in disruptive behavior. They are not able to stay in a situation and face something that is hard or demanding. Their actions show a lack of self-control.

Parents and teachers need to use tools and a common approach to support these children. We need to let them know that they can do more than they think they can, that it is okay just to try, and that the attempt is where the learning happens. As teachers, we spend a lot of time telling children what the benefit will be to finishing a hard task. We might use explicit reward systems; e.g., *If you finish your work, then you can go out for recess. If you work quietly, then you can earn extra free time.* We also try to explain natural consequences that occur from good work: *If you listen to the lesson, then you will know what to do once we begin the activity. If you add more detail to your story, then it will be stronger.* Day in and day out, we make little motivational speeches to our students as incentive or as warnings, often expressing them as *If/Then* statements. For some students these statements must be made explicitly and repeatedly, with very small task demands and very big immediate rewards. Other students have their own internal self-talk that leads them to get the hard stuff done. When asked, these students would say, "If I finish my work, then I can enjoy the free time that comes next," "I know that if I eat my apple, then I will get dessert," or "If I work hard, then I will do better in school.

How can we teach the kids their own *If/Then*s? How can we switch the dynamic so that it is not always an adult telling the child what needs to be done in order to achieve something? How can we establish systems that students can use to internalize life's daily balances of work-then-play? If a student is able to create their own *If/Then*s, they can make a start, move into a challenge, and try new approaches. When a student with this strategy in place is faced with unknowns, their internal thinking supports them to believe in themselves and to view challenges as part of the process. They have built-in strategies for persisting and overcoming: *Too bad, I guess I need to try something else. Not my favorite thing to do, but the faster I do it, the faster it will be finished.*

Practice-Based Learning

No matter what we do as teachers, we will have setbacks in class. Students detail their goals and outline their *If/Then* statements, but the challenging behavior repeats over and over again. We have to remember how hard it is to carry through with well-intentioned goals; for example, it is easy to have a goal to begin a diet, and we can have full belief that we can accomplish it, but it is hard to follow it at work or late at night when we are tired! Many students want to change their behavior and state that they believe they can do it. When they are calm, they can outline exactly what they should do in order to respond in the moment. But in class, during group work, or at recess, they find it difficult to maintain the positive self-talk and self-control needed in the moment, and the challenging behavior resumes.

In order to fully support students, we need to understand that imparting and nurturing a growth mindset and the strategies to maintain it is a long, slow process. It is hard for attitude and behavior to change quickly or easily. We need to understand that we can't make the changes for the child, that our job is simply to continue to play a supportive role, and repeat it as many times as necessary.

Helping Students Develop Practice Plans

As teachers, seeing the role of school as practice for setting goals and following through makes our roles in this process clearer. In sports or art practice, the coach or instructor sets out a lesson plan with the intention of using a set period to practice a few basic skills. When we work on something new, we break it down to its most basic steps and practice those steps over and over in isolation before we try to consolidate them with something we already know. During practice, we make mistakes, we drop the ball, we hit notes badly; we are working on things we do not know how to do. During practice, when we miss or drop something, we pick it up and try it again. That is how we learn. For performances or championship games, we are asked to perform at our best; the mistakes we make are seen by many and can disappoint others. Students with fixed mindsets are performing all the time. When they make mistakes, the weight of disappointment is on their shoulders. As teachers, we need to let students know that the classroom is a space for practicing. If we respond to challenging behavior as a coach would, making small corrections—for example, the way a player is holding the bat or the placement of a musician's fingers on the piano—then the student will be able to shift toward a growth mindset. They will recognize the value of slowing their bodies down, instead of being punished for going too fast. They will listen to the teacher feedback that suggests best strategies instead of ignoring the teachers' criticisms.

This process is best supported by daily language that lets students know you are not judging them, not constantly assessing them to give them a final mark. When you do give students tests, the language you choose will make a significant difference in the message you are sending them. A statement like "I want to see what you know," is based in fixed-mindset thinking; i.e., the test will show the knowledge the student has, how smart this student is. Instead, you could say, "I want to see what you know right now, so that we can decide what we will learn next." This statement is based in a growth mindset. Doing poorly on this test would not imply that the student is not smart; it simply reveals that more time needs to be spent working on that concept. (Johnston, 2012, p. 27)

See pages 29–30 for problem scales to use in categorizing and levelling problems.

We can encourage students to explore activities that they do well and enjoy doing. In these explorations, students reflect on their practice of these activities. They also reflect on how to handle setbacks during activities that they are good at and enjoy doing. During these preferred activities, they likely have a stronger mindset and use more self-control to push through challenges than they do during non-preferred activities. If they like the activity enough, they choose to practice and work on a specific drill over and over for a long period of time. Yet a student with a positive mindset and immense self-control in one area can have it all fall apart for something else. Students have areas of strength as well as areas of challenge, typically based on ability and interest. These influence the way they approach daily problems. To support students, many schools dedicate time to learning skills and character traits. Terms like *grit*, *empathy*, *organization*, and *self-regulation* are explained and these character traits are taught, both for students to develop them within themselves and to support others in behaving the same way.

Tools and Strategies

A growth mindset helps a person make choices that sustain the effort to move through challenges and to reach goals. It fosters the resilience to stick to goals despite setbacks, to keep going after you fail. These traits can be seen in very young children, who bounce back when things are hard. We want our students of any age to create an image of how they can respond when things are hard. Once they see how they would like to respond, the behavior they would like to engage in, then we can begin to examine strategies that can help them get there. With our help, students can create mental constructs that allow them to attempt hard things, push through, and engage in unpleasant tasks.

See Chapters 3 to 8 for more on the character traits that embody growth mindset and self-control.

We can assist students in figuring out how they can approach a task, so that they can face the unknown and put in the work to achieve something they want immediately. Then we can offer them an environment that will allow them to practice. We can expose them to tools and strategies that will help them successfully move through the hard parts. There are character traits that offer natural exposure and practice with the tools and strategies that shift mindsets and build self-control. Responsibility, Independence, Self-Regulation, Initiative, Perspective, and Resilience might be taught as separate character traits, but they are in fact different aspects of a bigger idea. Together these traits help students shift their self-talk so that it supports a growth mindset and develop the self-control needed to follow through with their *If/Then* statements.

2

Nurturing Growth in the Classroom

What do a growth mindset and self-control have in common? Children need both of them in order to succeed in school, at home, in extra-curricular activities, and in future accomplishments. A growth mindset is the thinking that success will come by being willing to do something that they don't love doing but that they know has value. This mindset tells children that they can begin a hard task and it is okay if they do not complete it perfectly. It allows them to believe that they can put something off they want immediately in order to move through a task, with the understanding that that in the end they will benefit from it. Self-control can be achieved with tools, specific strategies that support and enable a child to move through hard moments.

Explicit Teaching of Self-Control

In school, we deal with behavior and self-control challenges every day. While teaching math and language, while playing cooperative games, we are always trying to bring in students who do not want to participate. We are trying to support students to manage their behavior. More than teaching academics, we are supporting behavior day in and day out. How can we take what we are already doing and bring it into a cohesive approach? And how can we do it through existing curriculum?

Individuals level different problems differently. This is influenced by many factors.

If we examine the patterns of thinking and responding where they are strong, we can then apply that same thinking and responding in areas where they are not as successful.

- Some people have a predisposition toward growth mindset or optimistic thinking; these people view bumps in the day as something to tackle. Others, for whom a growth mindset does not come naturally, become overwhelmed, upset, stressed, or preoccupied with the bumps in the day.
- The activity itself will determine how a student responds to challenges in it. For example, when faced with an activity they like or are good at, a student will be more able to handle setbacks and challenges in the activity.
- The student's state that day is also important to consider: how much sleep they had the night before, the classroom temperature, things that have gone well or were challenging.
- Finally, you have to consider past experience: the ways in which the student has experienced other obstacles; whether they have faced them and moved through them or run from them; how they have been supported or not in facing them; etc.

As we become more aware of our strengths and struggles, we realize that the way we view challenges is not static. Depending on the activity, our responses to challenges can be very different. A student who yells, refuses to work, and never takes feedback when asked to write a story might be willing to observe a coach for hours, listen attentively to instruction, and practice a tricky hockey shot for hours. In class, a teacher might believe that this student has a closed mindset, weak work habits, or a negative attitude. But we have to be careful not to generalize. A child's most challenging behavior cannot be taken as representative of who the child is. Instead, we examine the student's approach to a challenge, figure out the student's thinking and response in circumstances when they are most successful, and apply all that we can learn about their thinking and response to areas where they are struggling to think and respond in optimistic ways. Students are less likely to be frustrated by setbacks when doing something they are good at. Moreover, if they face frustration while doing something they are good at, they tend to have more motivation to try to manage their responses.

We need to begin by helping students break down their challenges, struggles, or issues. With my students, I call these *problems*. We support them in examining their thinking and behavioral reactions around each challenge. Then we help them develop an *If/Then* statement to use to overcome the problem.

Breaking Down the Problem

We can help students reflect upon their problems and rate them, using a *problem scale*. Introducing your class to the problem scale helps them learn that everyone interprets problems in a different way, with a different mindset. If you look at many problems together as a class, over time you will develop the problem scale as a tool to help students gain perspective on the size of problems.

1. Draw a large problem scale on the board or interactive whiteboard. Place labels *Small* and *Large* on opposite ends; place a *Medium* label in the middle. See page 29 for the Problem Scale template.
2. Introduce the symbols used with the problem scale:

    Lightning bolt = the problem
    Thought bubble = what you think
    Speech balloon = what you say
    Square = action taken

3. Start with a clear example of a large problem that is likely not to be personally distressing to students; for example, dropping your mom's tablet and breaking it. This is a serious problem and most students would agree.
4. Use a lightning bolt to represent the problem and write the problem beside the lightning bolt:

    You break your mom's tablet.

5. Ask students where you should put this problem on the scale. Prompt: "Is this a small or tiny problem?" Most students will say no. Prompt: "Is this a medium-sized problem?" It's possible a few students will raise their hands. You could put a small lightning bolt on the scale at *Medium* to recognize their contribution. Prompt: "Who thinks this is a big or large problem?" When

Steps in Explicit Teaching of Self-Control
1. Using a problem scale, break down the problem by examining the student mindset and its influence on behavior.
2. Help students develop an *If/Then* statement to reflect a mindset that will allow them to overcome the problem.

I do not introduce the problem scale using real problems that occur during the day. Only once students have spent some time mastering the use of the problem scale would I use direct classroom examples.

most students raise their hands, place a larger lightning bolt in the scale at *Large*, but not at the very end of the scale. You want to show that there are larger problems than that.

6. Acknowledge that everyone rates problems differently, and that what might seem like a medium-sized problem to one person might be a small problem for others, and large problem to still others. Emphasize that we do not need to agree on the size of the problem, and leave both lightning bolts on the scale.

7. Continue scaling sample problems as a class until students are comfortable using the problem scale and rating their own perception of problems.

Examples of Problems

Problems that might be big:
- Dropping and breaking your tablet
- Getting suspended from school
- Having to do a presentation in front of the whole school
- Not being chosen for a team or a school performance
- Losing a championship game
- Your friend saying that they will never speak to you again and telling everyone not to talk to you
- Losing your whole computer file with your final presentation

Problems that might be medium-sized:
- Losing a regular-season game
- Not being allowed to go to a party
- Getting into a disagreement with a friend during a work project
- Losing a permission form
- Tripping and falling, but not getting hurt

Problems that might be small:
- Having no milk in the morning for cereal
- Missing a free-throw shot during basketball practice
- Having a friend tell you that you are speaking loudly and asking you to speak in a softer voice
- Tripping and almost falling
- Losing your weekly homework

---

8. Explain to students that problems can be moved along the problem scale as the problems get bigger or smaller. Show them the Problem Scale: Changing the Size of the Problem template from page 30.

9. Examine with students different actions they could take after the problem. Place these on the problem scale, using a square with each action written in it. Point out that some actions are quick and show a lack of self-control; they often make the problem bigger. Call them *reactions*. Then explain to students that there are actions we can take that will make the problem smaller; even though they might be small, they are often the hardest to do. These *responses* are controlled and deliberate.

Just because a response looks like something small to anyone watching does not mean that it is easy to do! Sometimes the smallest responses are the ones that take the most work because they require self-control.

Examples of Big Reactions and Controlled Responses

Big Reactions
- Kicking
- Punching
- Yelling hurtful messages
- Starting a horrible rumor and spreading it
- Ignoring and excluding someone

Controlled Responses
- Speaking in a quiet but forceful voice
- Walking away
- Explaining the problem from your point of view
- Doing nothing
- Seeking outside help to solve the situation

Valuing Students' Perceptions

What might be a big problem for some students would not be a problem at all for someone else. It is essential to empathize with children and their parents about the degree of seriousness and upset that a child attributes to a problem. If we undervalue the upset of one of our students, if we minimize the degree to which the student is bothered or stricken by a situation, then it is hard for us to be part of their journey toward self-improvement. If we judge a student's thinking and feeling before we start, then why would the child want to be part of an improvement process with us?

"This is not a big deal." "Let it go." "Some children around the world do not even get to go to school." These responses undermine a student's feelings and their right to their own feelings. The student's first reaction will be to justify why it is a problem, why they have the right to be upset. This will put further focus on the negative aspects of the event. Instead, you and the student should be developing together a thinking and action plan to help the student move through the upset.

Developing *If/Then* Statements

Once we have a clear understanding of the problem scale and are using it with our students, we can begin to develop with them *If/Then* sentences. These statements represent strategies that can help students understand how to tackle challenges and move through them, instead of giving up or being overwhelmed. In the Marshmallow Test (see page 10), most students wanted to wait for the second marshmallow, but only some of them knew what they needed to do in order to help themselves wait. Strategies exist that can help any child gain control over their behavior. We can teach our students these strategies.

1. Discuss with students the goals you have for the classroom. When deciding what goals are particularly important for your classroom, have students look at the problem scales created and consider if there are recurring issues or themes. If a lot of the lightning bolts represent students getting hurt or accidents happening, then point out to students that their actions may not be safe and careful. This might prompt the students to say that being safe is a goal. Examples of goals:

   - We need to be safe.
   - We want to be kind and supportive of our friends.
   - I want to work to the best of my abilities.

2. Take one problem you have on a problem scale and have students list what they might think to themselves if faced with that problem. Discuss with the class that they can focus on what is bad about the situation or they can think about ways to get around the obstacle. Chart the problem and the self-talk on the Mindset Chart on page 31, discussing and dividing the thinking into that which reflects a fixed mindset and that which reflects a growth mindset. Then have students list the behavior they would engage in based on their self-talk. Distinguish between a *reaction*, behavior that is done quickly or based on fixed-mindset self-talk, and a *response*, behavior that is controlled or based on growth-mindset self-talk.

SAMPLE MINDSET CHART

Obstacle/Problem *When I move around the classroom, I bump into others.*	
Fixed-Mindset Self-Talk	Fixed Mindset Reactions
"I can't help it." "They should move out of my way." "It's their fault if they get hurt." "It's their fault if I get hurt."	• stay in your seat • blame someone else and yell at them • cry • sulk
Growth-Mindset Self-Talk	Growth Mindset Responses
"There are lots of things I can do to be more careful."	• slow down • keep my arms and legs in • be aware of where my body is and where the bodies of others are

3. Introduce students to *If/Then* statements. Using the chart you filled out as a class in step 2, combine fixed-mindset self-talk with reactions:

   If I think that I can't help it, ***then*** I will stay in my seat.
   If I think that others should move out of my way, ***then*** I will sulk if they don't.
   If I think it's someone else's fault if they get hurt, ***then*** I will yell at them.
   If I think it's someone else's fault if I get hurt, ***then*** I will cry.

Using the chart, combine growth-mindset self-talk with controlled responses:

Mindset and self-control are interconnected. They are both essential aspects of success, but neither one is enough without the other. Without the belief that they can do it, a student will not attempt to do the hard tasks; without exposure to tools and strategies that lead to successful outcomes, the student cannot be successful even if they believe they can be.

If I think about being more careful, ***then*** I will slow down.
If I think about being more careful, ***then*** I will keep my arms and legs in.
If I think about being more careful, ***then*** I will be aware of where my body is and where the bodies of others are.

4. Tell students that now we want to make sure that *Ifs* give explicit thinking or behaviors. For example, this statement implies behavior instead of describing it: *If we are safe, then no one will get hurt.* This *If* does not give a specific goal or thing to work on in order to be safe; therefore, it is not likely to get a positive result. Most students would agree that we want to be safe, but they are not always able to manage their reactions in the moment; their uncontrolled reactions can result in someone getting hurt. Help students detail explicit behavior:

   To be safe:
   - Keep my hands and feet to myself.
   - Move slowly around the classroom.
   - Be aware of where my body is and where the bodies of others are.

   To be kind and supportive:
   - Smile at our friends and use a soft voice.
   - Be attentive when someone else is speaking.
   - Try not to move around when someone is talking to us.
   - Face our friends and look at them when they are talking.
   - Nod in encouragement and understanding.

   To work to the best of my abilities:
   - Try things even when they are hard.
   - Try different ways of doing things.
   - Ask for help from others only after I have tried myself.

   A strong *If/Then* statement might be this: *If we walk slowly down the stairs, then we will be less likely to fall.*

When students who demonstrate little motivation and rarely want to do anything create fixed-mindset *Thens*, it is important not to halt their participation in the process by correcting them. Celebrate their plan and slowly shift their *Thens* to ones that reflect a growth mindset.

5. Develop *Thens*, focusing on practice-based learning. Help students see that some *Thens* are based on a fixed mindset, with a focus on the end result or reward: e.g., praise from the teacher, not being yelled at by another student, not getting hurt. With the class, brainstorm *Thens* that are based on a growth mindset, focusing on the process and effort: e.g., learning how to control my body, making the classroom safer for myself and others. Ideally, *Thens* reflect that students have learned something, practiced, tried harder, and pushed themselves even when it was hard. These *Thens* have intrinsic value; they ultimately lead to more self-development and support daily exposure that can shift mindsets.

Even if students are taught these strategies, they will not be able to implement them immediately. There is considerable distance between knowing what to do and being able to do it.

Assessment *Thens*

It can be hard to know what to do when an *If/Then* relates to assessment: e.g., *If I write one more sentence, then I will get a Level 4.* You would need to think about your goals for this child. Can this child accept feedback? Some students, if they receive too much direction or feedback, will shut down. If you try to alter the *If/Then*, the student might lose motivation. Is it worth shutting down the process because you know that the student is not going to get a Level 4? You might consider creating an individual rubric with the student for that particular day or task; i.e., to find success and give a level 4 for one sentence. It is something you can build on: for the next day, the student will have to write two sentences for that Level 4!

---

5. Use the problem scale to connect *If/Then* statements to mindset. A student's mindset and the self-talk they use can move the problem along the scale. Use a lightning bolt to show the problem and a thought bubble for self-talk. You can write directly on the thought bubble and tape it to the problem scale, or you can move the thought bubble along the scale when the student says the thought, showing the problem as becoming bigger or smaller:

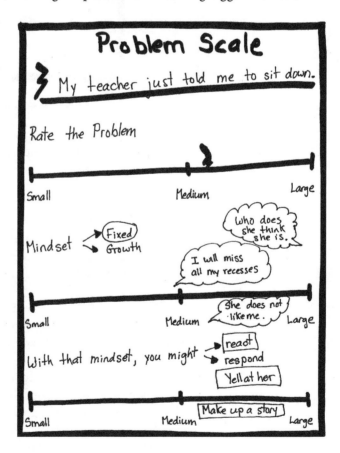

We can see how a fixed mindset and negative self-talk can make the problem bigger.

But students with a growth mindset, using positive self-talk, can make the problem smaller:

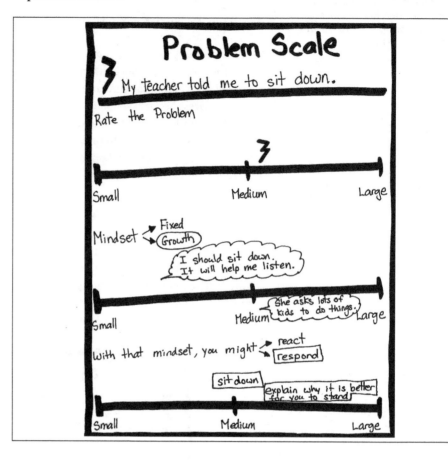

A student's self-talk after a problem will determine future feelings and actions. We can encourage students to examine and reflect on daily challenges as we guide their interpretation of challenges. Together we can make a plan that will foster the growth mindset. This mindset will allow them to understand that the problem is not as huge as it feels, as well as the self-control needed to be able to respond to the problem in a successful way. Self-talk strategies help them remember that the problem is not as big as they felt it was. Show students they can use self-talk to create *If/Thens*:

- If I tell myself, "Sometimes I face problems during the day. That is okay; everyone does," then my problem will not seem so big.
- If I tell myself, "I can handle this," then I might be able to get through it.

6. Encourage students to reflect on the things they have done in the past that have made a problem bigger. Make sure they know they can think about these times without feeling guilty or embarrassed. Instead, they can remember these times to try to figure out what to do differently. Negative *If/Then* statements can be used to determine the sort of self-talk and mindset that have exacerbated a problem:

- *If I scream at the teacher when she asks me to use a quiet voice, then I will be asked to write a letter of apology for being rude.*

- *If I push my friend when they will not play the game that I want, then they will be mad at me.*
- *If I push my desk over when I am asked to sit down and write five sentences, then I will have to clean up during recess.*

Negative *If/Then*s can be replaced by positive If/Thens that will make a problem smaller:

- *If I take one step away from my friend when they are bothering me, then I will not keep making the problem bigger.*
- *If I sit down and write my sentences, then I can go outside and play with my friends.*
- *If I stop yelling at a classmate for making noise in the classroom, then the room will be quieter because I am not making noise too.*

Internalizing the Growth Mindset

Provide insight to students on their role in problems and the power they have in their own lives; they should not be looking to an adult to help, to fix, to be their problem-solver. With information, we empower students to see themselves as the cause of their positive outcomes because they have control over their success. We can start by presenting students with *If/Then*s and demonstrating a growth mindset, but our ultimate goal is for students to internalize and take ownership of their own growth mindset and positive self-talk. There will not always be an adult there, ready to repeat and negotiate tangible rewards. But if students create their own *If/Then* scenarios, we can offer them support to see them through.

The Benefit of Rewards

For toddlers and young children, the benefit from doing something challenging or boring is often a tangible, external reward. They need to see a clear reward or incentive and it needs to come quickly and immediately. We can't say to a four-year-old, "If you sit down and write all morning, then tomorrow you can play outside." The demand is too great and the reward too far away. We support young students by asking them to do something small and following it immediately with a tangible reward; e.g., "First, you write your name, then you can go to the sand table. "

In life, there is always a reward. It might not always be as external as a marshmallow, stickers, candies, or extra TV, but it is there. Some students understand implicit rewards and work toward them: *If I work hard, then I will learn something. If I help clean up the room, then I will demonstrate that I am a helpful student. If I finish a hard assignment, then I can be proud of myself for doing something challenging.* These students like to see a finished product that is well done. They like it when the teacher looks at their work and tells them they've done a good job. However, other students don't understand or are not as motivated by implicit rewards. For these students, we need to be much more explicit about our expectations and the rewards that follow.

Recess as Reward

As teachers, we want our students to go out for recess. Children need time for physical activity and fun. But consider that it is okay to present recess in the context that it is *not* a given. Recess is put into the schedule as a break after a period of hard work; we get recess because we have worked hard. If a student has not worked or has been disruptive, then they have not earned their break. They have not completed the school's *If/Then* mandate: *If we do our morning work, then we get our break.* If a student has played during work time, *then* does it not make sense that they need to work during play time?

There are natural consequences in life. *If* you do not meet a reasonable expectation, *then* you do not get the rewards that come after. We are not doing students any favors by depriving them of an understanding of expectations and natural consequences in life.

In order to implement an incentive system, a teacher needs to have a very strong understanding of what every child is capable of. All students cannot do the same task in order to get a reward. In writing, all students cannot be asked to complete a whole page in order to get recess. During a lesson, all students cannot listen for the same amount of time, but there should still be an achievable goal that every child is working toward in order to receive their reward.

As we explicitly teach children that they get something positive if they work hard, we are teaching them self-control. We need to help them take ownership of this approach and internalize self-talk that allows them to set their own *If/Then* statements: *If I do something hard, then I will benefit in the end. If I work hard, then I will be more successful in the end.*

It is important to understand what that kind of success looks like. Success does not necessarily mean achieving a Level 4 or an A+; it doesn't mean being the best at something. Success is trying something hard, continuing to work through obstacles, and completing a job in its entirety. It is doing a little bit better than you did yesterday. It is trying something today that you did not want to try yesterday. It is taking a new step, using a different approach, or having a more positive outlook on something than you had the day before. That is success.

Practice-Based Learning

As teachers, we sometimes feel overwhelmed by curriculum and new initiatives on our plate.

In the past, I found myself spending a lot of time talking with students about their behavior, the choices they were making every day, and the way those choices affected the functioning of our classroom as a whole. While those discussions were essential for students and supported them in the classroom, I wanted to be better able to integrate them into what I was doing in my teaching practice. How can we use what we are already doing in class, in language, in drama, and in math, to support the teaching of behavior and learning strategies that last a lifetime?

Create a Safe Space

Classrooms can be a safe place for unknowns and problem-solving, as long as we set them up to offer a base structure of routines and reliability. There need to be bins and places for materials that are accessible to students and chosen by students. This creates an order that can be maintained, something I call the *rhythm of the class*. There is a movement through learning that is predictable and safe.

Within that structure, great learning can take place as children face unknowns and uncertainties. I do not tell each student where to place their language folder or where they can put the extra project they brought in for a special occasion. I frequently pause to wonder with my students what we should do or where they think the learning might go. These moments of uncertainty, demonstrating the lack of exact right or wrong answers, allow students to sense that the world has grey areas in it. There might not be a right way and a wrong way to do something; there may be a few different ways. And that is pretty cool!

Let Students Lead

An important aspect of setting up a classroom that nurtures a growth mindset is that most of the elements are created by the students. Anchor charts should not be store-bought or written in perfect teacher writing. Student work and student writing should be all over the classroom. It is okay to have posters on the walls that have some spelling mistakes if they are made by students; it is even better to have corrections made by students on those posters. This exemplifies the learning process, the ability to make mistakes and be willing to correct them.

Consider this:
- Would you rather have a store-bought map of the world in your classroom or an imperfect map made by your students?
- Would you rather clean up yourself or have students spill paint all over the floor and clean it up badly, but do it themselves?
- Would you rather set up book club tables and get reading books for your students during every recess or have them take time out of reading groups to move their desks and look for books to read?
- Would you rather cover up a mistake you made and try to convince your class that they misunderstood you or admit that you were wrong?

A perfectly teacher-led classroom promotes a fixed mindset. Growth mindsets allow for mistakes, imperfections, and critical review. The fact that a teacher makes a mistake does not take away from the teacher's strength. The self-reflection and ability to identify other options for response is what makes a strong teacher.

Be sure to support some projects that are open-ended, even imperfect. Detailing each aspect of a project can take away opportunities for problem-solving and imperfection. Open-endedness might lead to chaotic moments in the room, when 15 students are asking you questions, unsure of what to do and how to do it. But seeing these moments through, day in and day out, is mindset practice. It builds the experience of facing unknowns and moving through them.

Your classroom calendar can be made by students. The first time they make it, all the dates will likely be wrong, but you can refer to a calendar with them and make the changes.

Develop a practice-based teaching plan that integrates your classroom's daily challenges and obstacles into your practice. Instead of viewing daily problems as issues that distract from your teaching, build your curriculum lesson plans around the concepts of mindset and self-control. And use any disagreement or unknown *as* the lesson, instead of seeing it as interrupting the lesson.

Strategies and Activities

Oral Language

A primary purpose of oral language is to teach communication. Communication involves listening to the thoughts and ideas of others and expressing one's own thoughts and ideas. Being able, as a class, to discuss problems and challenges facilitates growth-mindset discussions about moving through those problems and trying to make them smaller.

A daily check-in is a wonderful way to promote class harmony, to model ways of interacting positively, to catch and work through classroom social struggles, and to set up a positive classroom discussion dynamic. All this is done while covering oral-language curriculum. Ideally, these discussions take the form of a sharing circle: everyone is equal, there is no leader or teacher at the head; all students are part of the circle. Peer sharing is often used as an extension of the circle. It saves time and gives everyone a chance to add their voice. When you begin to think that the needs of all students are not being met, ask a question and tell students to turn to the student next to them to share their thoughts on the answer..

Reading

First students learn to read, then they read to learn. Book-club and guided reading activities let students choose books to read with their peers for the purpose of learning to read, then for the purpose of gathering information. When students stumble over words together, then support each other in sounding out the words, they are experiencing practice-based learning as a group. With teacher support, students can begin to seek out books just above their reading level, as peers will help them with unknown words. I call this level Just Right with Friends, a level higher than the reading level that is Just Right on Their Own; academically, this is called the Zone of Proximal Development. This is the level at which we want to be reaching our students. The reading is a little hard for them and does not come easily, but with work it is achievable. Read-alouds offer opportunities for students to practice reading at their Just Right on Their Own level and to share their reading with the class. This process teaches students the value of practicing and putting effort into something. Silent reading allows children to experience the benefits of relaxation through an activity and the joy of reading self-selected books.

Writing

We can tie everything we are working on with students into their writing process. By using writing as a significant tool in our program, we cover essential aspects of the curriculum while targeting social-emotional needs and having students examine mindsets. When planning your writing program, begin with the idea of a growth mindset and ensure that your topics, images, and graphic organizers reflect self-control.

Teach and expand your students' writing by showing them how to develop strong characters, voice, and interest. Use your teacher e-mail account to have students write to their parents during the day. Not only will this improve their writing and let them work on typing skills, but it also importantly increases the level of communication between you and the parents through your students, instead of around them.

I often scooch myself over to sit with a group I think will need my support in making sure each student gets a turn and shares ideas. I also often try to sit near, but not in the same group as, a student who does not often contribute to large classroom discussions. It is great to be able to hear the child's voice.

Use rich social-emotional texts to support students in critically thinking about perspectives that are the same as and different from their own.

Media Studies

When planning media studies, begin with the big idea of growth mindset and reflect on aspects of self-control as you have students express a message or point of view to others. Once you discuss goals, promises, and expectations in class, get students capture what you discuss as a group through a variety of media texts for different purposes and audiences, using appropriate forms, conventions, and techniques.

Math

Use data management to collect and analyze students' mindsets, thoughts, feelings, and actions. You can use the surveys in this book or make up questions of your own that reflect the challenges in your classroom. Begin to encourage students to design their own surveys and questionnaires. Be sure to review questions before they are asked to ensure that they are not too personal.

Art/Drama

Reinforce the idea that presentations can be a form of practice instead of a final performance by using activities that involve learning to work in front of others in a safe space. Students should be able to try things and redo them. Show the students that they are not being judged.

Use role play to allow students to explore thoughts, feelings, and actions that would be the result of the different scenarios. Drama imagination activities can be done during circle discussions, with students closing their eyes and being prompted to imagine the thoughts, feelings, and actions of another; e.g., a character from a book, someone from real life. Create a scenario, situation, or problem and prompt students to describe it as if they were someone else or as if they were watching a character go through this problem.

Homework Activities

Growth mindsets and self-control are not just for the classroom. The traits and skills presented in this book are equally valuable for a child's life outside of school. Use homework to engage with parents at home. Share mindset and self-control information with parents by explicitly detailing the language you use and classroom expectations; one of the best ways to do this is through aspects of their child's homework. Show parents direct ways they can support their children at home. Create a homework atmosphere that promotes the idea that all students are working on different things.

With communication and goal-setting, parents and teachers can determine a homework program that is flexible, consistent, and achievable, one that is specific for each child and targets something the child needs to work on every night. Parents are often much more open and on-board when they see what they and their children are doing as being meaningful.

Homework systems that assign no homework for weeks, then an enormous amount of homework in one night, do not build stamina. Families need a repetitive process that is manageable and predictable, so that they can build it into their routine and alter it depending on their needs.

Mindset Rubrics

Link classroom activities to a goal-setting rubric in order to make each step as explicit as possible. As we try to encourage students to take risks and go outside their comfort zone, some of them need explicit action steps that guide their behaviors. Students with fixed mindsets can become paralyzed with uncertainty about what to do next, about which step is okay to take. If we implement choice-based classrooms and open-ended activities without a strong and safe base of clear goals, many students can become lost in the choices and unknowns.

I use rubrics in every aspect of my program to establish expectations. They also help students self-assess their work, set goals, and add to and apply previous learning to their next work. A rubric allows students to see examples of their own work and that of others that do not hit the goal, that almost do, that hit the goal, and that surpass it. With explicit detail, students can see examples, for all aspects of life, of what to do and what not to do. As well as being useful in academic assessment, rubrics can highlight ways to approach a task, to think about a task, to begin a task. The strength of a rubric lies in its explicit detail and visual examples of behavior. Using explicit steps that students can see, it helps them pinpoint the thinking or behavior they can try next.

Help your students embed rubrics into everything they do: their approach to tasks and the process of the task itself.

SAMPLE RUBRIC

Level 1	Level 2	Level 3	Level 4
Try again	Keep trying	That is it	You did more
You might want to try something else.	If you keep trying and doing more of the same thing, you will get it.	You got it. It is exactly what it was supposed to be.	You took it to another level. You did something new, interesting, and creative. You could teach it to others.

Problem Scale

No ——— Small ——— Medium ——— Large ——— Huge

0 ——— 5 ——— 10

Pembroke Publishers ©2017 *Keep Growing* by Joey Mandel ISBN 978-1-55138-320-0

Problem Scale: Changing the Size of the Problem

Describe the problem:

_____

Rate the problem.

```
|----------------------|----------------------|
Small                Medium                 Large
```

Mindset → Fixed
Mindset → Growth

```
|----------------------|----------------------|
Small                Medium                 Large
```

With that mindset you might → react
With that mindset you might → respond

```
|----------------------|----------------------|
Small                Medium                 Large
```

Pembroke Publishers ©2017 *Keep Growing* by Joey Mandel ISBN 978-1-55138-320-0

Mindset Chart

Obstacle/Problem	

Fixed Mindset Self-Talk	Fixed Mindset Reactions

Growth Mindset Self-Talk	Growth Mindset Responses

3

Responsibility

Responsibility

What it is: The ability to begin, move through, and complete tasks, activities, and jobs that you should do, but may not want to do. A willingness to follow rules and schedules for the greater good. Taking accountability for actions and choices.

What it looks like:

- Following the routines of the classroom.
- Listening when someone else is speaking.
- Slowing your body down so that you can sit and listen.
- Organizing your desk.
- Keeping track of your belongings.
- Being able to acknowledge mistakes you made or things you wish you had not done.
- Making mistakes and changing your behavior so that the same mistakes do not happen the next time.
- Doing assigned homework.

As children begin to face daily challenges, they begin a response process of mindset and self-control. During daily decision-making and responses, will they have a clear sense of what behaviors are helpful for themselves and others? Children need to truly understand good choices and their responsibilities to themselves and others, so that they can support positive classroom communities. We want to promote growth mindsets that help our students to understand their responsibility toward themselves and others, to make choices that de-escalate problems, and to support their self-control with the tools that allow them to modify their behavior.

Rules and boundaries are the very things that guide children to limit and manage their behavior. In order to be responsible, children need to know explicitly what that means and what it looks like. They need to know what they should and should not do for any activity, in any situation. They must be motivated and able to comply with expectations that are set around them. Then they need the tools and strategies that help them to resist in the moment the choices and temptations that would take them off-task. Finally, and most importantly, when children do not follow the rules and are given a consequence for poor choices or mistakes, they need a consistent process for receiving the feedback given to them, for taking what they have learned into the next time. Will they give up and continue to make poor choices, or will they learn from their missteps and change their behavior? As we create a classroom environment based in responsibility, we can help shift students' mindsets, develop their self-control, and change their subsequent behavior.

Responsibility in the Classroom

Rules are the primary way that we support students in recognizing what they are responsible for. Co-created classroom rules are important steps toward setting up expectations, as they invite students to be a part of their own goal-setting. Students create *If/Then* self-talk statements that will motivate them and help them set their own limits.

Once we have created rules as a classroom, the hard work actually begins. There will be some students who will never violate a rule all year. There are others who will break a few, and then take ownership of their mistakes or bad choices and try hard not to break those rules again. Some students might break many classroom rules each day. Some of the students who repeatedly break the rules will be upset with themselves, even feel guilty. They might run away or avoid the next tasks. Their moods might shift. Other students who break daily rules hardly seem to be aware of what they have done and might seem not to care. Still others will be outraged at the teacher's response to the broken rule, becoming angry and hurt that someone would approach them and want to discuss their behavior.

How do we shift this process so that the teacher is not responsible for chasing each behavior? How do we make students responsible for what they do? How do we encourage students to take ownership for the rules and their following of them? How do we help our students be accountable to themselves and their process, rather than to us as teachers? It is easy to create classroom rules; however, it can be difficult to support the students who do not follow them. Support students in setting their own individual goals from the list of classroom rules. Encourage them to

- identify classroom rules they think they can follow well
- identify classroom rules they think might sometimes be hard for them
- identify classroom rules they think might often be hard for them

The Marshmallow Test (page 10) showed us that some children have a predisposition toward the self-control needed to delay gratification. These children have a naturally positive *If/Then* perspective that helps them more easily and willingly do something hard. In class, this same perspective can help students naturally engage in tasks in expectation of a reward. Rather than a tangible object or physical reward, the student might earn the knowledge of doing what they think is the right thing or of making others happy. Children who are more successful in terms of their life and social skills are internally motivated with all kinds of positive life *If/Thens*: *If I do my work, I will get to go out for recess. If I do my work, the teacher will notice and will tell me that I am doing a great job.*

Some specialists insist that we should never discuss the negatives; we should outline behavior only and always in a positive way; we should show students what we want them to do, not highlight and draw their attention to undesirable behavior. I believe that some things cannot be fully understood until the student can examine a situation from all angles. Once children truly understand the full consequences they face for negative behavior, then they can be motivated to try to adjust their behavior.

Often behavior contracts make a teacher's work more difficult, as they likely involve different tracking systems and different rewards for each child. We want to come up with a process in which the reward is student-driven, placing the ownership with the student.

If a student's *Then* involves getting praise from others, try to gradually change the *Then* so it is based on the student's acknowledgment of their own achievement.

The possibilities for *If/Then* statements are endless, but the goal is that they represent natural consequences of life. If the same student never cleans up the classroom, then they will frustrate the teacher and the other students. If a student does not contribute to group work, then another student might get upset. If a student is playing during work time, then the teacher might say that they are being unfair by interrupting the learning of others. If a student excludes others at recess, then they may get a low mark in cooperation on their report card.

The goal in these strategies is to slowly and kindly, but realistically, help children understand their behavior and the consequences of their behavior. The goal is to help them create their own *If/Then* statements that will motivate them to delay gratification and to begin, move through, and complete hard or unpleasant tasks.

A Practice-Based Learning Environment for Responsibility

1. Support students in reflecting on problems that are occurring in the classroom and use them to co-create classroom rules and goals.
2. Have the students use those rules to create their *If/Then* statements that will give them explicit information to help them successfully follow the rules.
3. Give students multiple opportunities to use their *If/Then* statements to make problems smaller and follow the classroom rules.

Strategies and Activities

Oral Language: Sharing Circle

Tips for Sharing Circles

Take the time to set the circle properly.

- Always ensure that there is room for everyone in the circle. Students who are left out of circle may be the students who are left out of other group activities.
- Model to all students how to notice someone outside the circle and how to move over to make room for them, and how to prompt them to move their bodies into the circle.
- Establish as a class priority that everyone's body (shoulders and head facing in) is a part of the circle.
- If students look at and talk to the teacher only, prompt them to share their story with the whole class, to look around the whole circle:

You are sharing your story with everyone, not just me, so it is important that you look at everyone.

If needed, use more explicit prompts to explain:

If you just look at me when you are sharing your story, then other students in the class might stop listening to you when you speak. They might think that what you are saying is just for the teacher and not for them. When you speak in class, it is important to look around at everyone so that everyone in the class is included in your story.

- Remind students to treat others the way they would like to be treated. That means listening quietly and not talking.
- Establish patterns for student interaction. Every teacher action influences how students respond to each other. Any time we are unkind to a student, laugh at them, or show our frustration, students take on that same behavior with each other. Each time we are kind to a student, respond with a smile to one who sits in an odd way, picks their nose, or says something off-topic, we model thoughtful responses.

1. Use a sharing circle to work with students to create *If/Then* statements about classroom interactions. Have students step into the circle if they agree with the statement.

   - If I do not try as hard as I can in the running race, then I may come in last.
   - If I practice my basketball shots every day, then I will get more shots in.
   - If I stop trying, then kids who are not as skilled as I am but try harder may beat me.
   - If I carry too many things down the stairs and fool around, then I could fall down the stairs and get hurt.
   - If I talk during someone's presentation, then they might think that I am rude.
   - If I tell someone they can't play with me at recess, then they may call me a bully.

   We can then use this process with students to draw their attention to the fact that there are consequences for actions.

If the problem scale is near your circle, you can take a lightning bolt symbol and place it on the scale between Small and Medium.

2. Discuss with students that these are small or medium-sized problems; see page 16 for more on problem scales. They are problems we may not want, but they are not huge. We then have choices so that the medium or small problems do not recur.

3. Turn the discussion to individual responsibilities and classroom routines. Ask students to step into the circle if they agree with the statement.

   - If I do not work during work time, then I will have to work during play time.
   - If I work my hardest during classroom time, then I will earn my recess.
   - If I add more detail, then my writing will likely be better.
   - If I work harder on my project, then it should be more interesting.
   - If I help clean up the classroom, then people will think that I am helpful.

4. Ask students to consider what *If/Then* statements would work for them. Have students create other *If/Then* statements that link an action to a consequence.

Reading: Guided Reading

September is about establishing routines and rules of the classroom. Use the concept of responsibility to help your class set up centres and guided reading groups to maximize success. If you begin your reading groups too quickly, without enough explicit behavioral instructions, then you may struggle with the level of noise in your class and amount of work students are getting done all year.

1. Set up Guided Reading for success by explicitly outlining the work process with students. Ask them to brainstorm Reading Group responsibilities and rules. Then have them suggest *If/Then* statements for each rule:

2. As a group, create meaningful *If/Then* statements that will detail what you hope to achieve as a group.

   - If we try to read words, even when they are hard, then we will slowly improve our reading together.
   - If we face our friends and try to look at them when they are talking, then we will listen to each other better.

Writing: E-mail

As teachers, we do not want to limit our communication with parents to when things are going poorly. However, it can be hard to keep up with all the communication parents might feel they need. We can have students help us maintain communication with their parents. Have students e-mail their parents from school, detailing aspects of their day.

Since the e-mail will be sent to parents from your account, be sure to make it clear that the message is from their child. Use the student's name in the subject heading.

1. Celebrate first! Have students draft an e-mail to their parents to say what they have done well.

   - Today I read a new DRA book. Now I am at Level 12. I am so excited about this!
   - I got my book report back today and my teacher said that I wrote a detailed summary of the book. I got a Level 4!

2. We can model growth-mindset thinking by including details that shift the success from product to process. Have students reflect on the learning or the process of something they are celebrating. Encourage them to add an *If/Then* statement.

   - I am excited about this, because it means that my nightly reading is starting to pay off. If I keep reading at home, then my reading will continue to improve.
   - Thanks, Mom, for encouraging me to sit down and continue working on the report. If I continue to work hard by sitting down, starting my work, and following the rubric, then I can get a Level 4 again. It was worth it. See you tonight.

For more information on sentence walls and a variety of samples, check out my Read and Spell Well Program on the Teachers Pay Teachers website.

Using Sentence Walls

Some students struggle to organize their thoughts and to summarize classroom time. I have found that sentence walls are an effective tool to support student writing without creating dependence on them. Sentence walls are like word walls, but instead of isolated words around the room, sentence walls use patterned writing and provide students with key words that are applicable to what they are writing.

---

3. Use the Sentence Wall: E-mail Home on page 42 as a sentence wall or model to support the writing structure of e-mails and to shift responsibility for writing from you to students.
4. After a few positive e-mails, you can begin to have students send their parents e-mails for not-so-great times, to let them know that something went badly during the day. Students can explain the event from their point of view; because you are there, their point of view may be less one-sided than it would be if they went home and explained their troubles on their own.

> • Hi, Dad. I had a medium-sized problem at school today. I did not want to do any work so I ran out of the classroom.
> • Hi, Mom. Today I had a biggish problem. I hurt my friend. I wish that I walked away when people were telling me that I could not play. But I did not. I hit my friend. If I walk away when people are telling me that I can't play, then I will not get as mad and make a bad choice.

Media Studies: One-Rule Posters

As teachers, it is essential to understand that all aspects of daily classroom life are easy for some students and hard for others. This includes academic and social-emotional aspects. We can't have a framework that operates on the assumption that students who comply in class and behave "well" are trying harder or are nicer than those who don't. Classroom posters should convey clear messages about the thinking and the behavior that is involved in some of our implicit assumptions. We can't just tell children to be responsible. We need to break down what that looks like and how they can do it.

1. With students, brainstorm a classroom rule, goal, or message.
2. Model with students the need for explicit rather than implicit information. For example, use this general rule: *We need to listen.* Discuss why listening is important:

> If we listen to our friends, we will learn something that we did not know before.

Discuss details of what listening looks like:

> Listening means
> • Stopping what we are doing
> • Turning our head toward the person who is speaking
> • Looking at the person who is speaking

3. As you co-construct messages for the students, start creating two posters on the interactive whiteboard or on large pieces of paper. Make mistakes: e.g., spelling mistakes, missed capitals, inconsistent lettering, messy writing, illegible writing. If students say nothing, continue writing and co-constructing. If the students give you feedback, correct as you go.
4. Once you have finished, ask students to give you feedback. What is good about each poster? What needs work?
5. Create a quick rubric with student input.

Encourage students to use the problem scale and create an *If/Then* statement. But do not rush this. It is important to implement this language slowly, so that students do not become overwhelmed by it. The goal of the e-mail is sometimes just for a student to sit down and type a note to their parents.

I try not to have students make posters from new Bristol board or card stock. Provide the back of posters or cardboard from boxes that you plan to recycle. This helps reduce your classroom expense and is a great way to model environmental awareness. More importantly, reused materials tend not to be as perfect or shiny. It can be helpful for students who are perfectionists to begin with material that is imperfect.

Explicit detail needs to be repeated over and over before students can begin to change mindset and develop self-control.

Level 1	Level 2	Level 3	Level 4
Rushed it	Good enough	Makes the point well	Makes the point well Convinces the viewer
Hard to read	Clear	Neat and legible	Neatly written Uses different colors and fonts
Lots of mistakes	A few mistakes	One or two minor mistakes	No mistakes
No detail	Little detail	Uses details and visuals	Uses detailed language Has graphics that explain the information

6. Once you have evaluated the posters with the students, ask them if you should consider them finished or move it up a level. Use the rubric to improve the posters. Fix the spelling mistakes with them, make the printing neater, and add detail and graphics.
7. With students working in pairs, have each pair pick one of the posters you have made and make a copy of the same poster. Challenge students to try to make their poster one level higher than yours.

SAMPLE PROCESS

Implicit	Explicit
I am responsible for myself. I am responsible for my own behavior. • I do not worry about what other people are doing. • I make sure that I am doing what I am supposed to do during the day. • I follow the class rules.	I follow class rules by waiting my turn when someone is talking, by listening to them speak. I do not move around when they speak. I stop, plant my feet, turn to them and listen to their words. I do not speak over them. When they are done talking, I comment on what they say. I follow class rules by waiting my turn in line. I go to the back of the line and am ready to wait for awhile. If the line is long, I think inside my head, "What else could I do while I wait in this line?" I might entertain myself by singing a song in my head, counting in my head, or telling myself a story. If I am waiting in line for the teacher to help me, I think about other ways to solve the problem than by waiting for the teacher to help me.

I follow the rules is a general statement. There is too much implied information. There are many rules and ways to follow those rules. Detailed explanations of how to wait your turn contains explicit information.

WE WILL LISTEN TO EACH OTHER
LISTENING LOOKS LIKE THIS STOP In order to listen, I can stop talking. In order to listen, I can stop moving around. TURN In order to listen, I can turn toward the person who is speaking. In order to listen, my face can look toward their face. NOD In order to show that I am ready to listen, I can nod. In order to listen, I can pay attention when the person is speaking. RESPOND In order to show that I am listening, I can comment on what my friend says. In order to show that I am listening, I will talk about them not about myself.
If I listen to other people, then when I talk, they will listen to me!

Math: Self-Assessment Survey

Have students collect, investigate, and organize personal data by creating a simple self-assessment survey. Students love to create their own questions and design surveys that are meaningful to themselves and their experience. Encourage them to gather and analyze information about aspects of their thinking and behavior that affects the classroom.

No one is asking students to be perfect all the time. But using the self-awareness that some rules are harder to follow, we can start to set goals and create practice-based learning opportunities for our students.

1. Have students list possible grade-appropriate classroom rules.
2. Explain that you understand that most students want to follow the rules, but that it is easier for some students to follow the rules than others. Knowing the rules does not mean that everyone knows how to follow them or how to make themselves follow them in the moment.
3. Get data that examines how easy or hard it is for students to follow the rules. Have each student review and reflect on the classroom rules and routines, then fill out a chart.

SAMPLE PRIMARY RULES CHART

Rule	Easy for me.	Hard for me, but I can do it.	Very hard for me, so I might not always be able to do it.
Don't talk during lessons.			
Begin work right away.			

Look at the sheet of paper to see if there is an example before asking for help.			
Wait my turn.			
Use a soft voice during centres.			
Help to clean up the room.			

SAMPLE JUNIOR RULES

Rule	Easy for me.	Hard for me, but I can do it.	Very hard for me, so I will likely not always be able to do it.
Be quiet during a lesson.			
Begin work right away.			
Read the sheet twice before asking for help.			
Begin work before asking for help.			
First complete the parts of the sheet that I can do.			
Listen to others when they talk.			
Compromise with others during group assignments.			
Consider different sides of a problem.			

Art/Drama: Tableau

I never begin the year with students acting full role-play scenarios, as they can lead to too much movement and silliness in the classroom. I tend to focus on a tableau pose that captures the reaction of the *Then* part of the *If/Then* statement. Or I have students state their *Then* in a voice that reflects the mood of the result of the statement.

Students need to learn that it is okay to examine natural negative consequences in life. We want to help students understand that these setbacks, challenges, even failures are opportunities to learn and grow. In order to create positive *If/Then* statements, we need to examine possible negative outcomes of *If/Then*s: e.g., *If* I eat the marshmallow right away, *then* I will not get a second one.

1. Draw a problem scale on the whiteboard; see page 29 for the template.

    If I yell at the teacher when she asks me to do my work, then I will have to write a reflection sheet over recess.

2. Read out *If/Then* prompts. Ask students to place a lightning bolt somewhere on the problem scale to mark how big the problem is.

> If I hurt my friend, then they will feel sad.
> If I steal money, then I will be someone who does dishonest things.
> If I wreck something that belongs to my classmate, then I could get caught.
> If I do not do my homework, then I am not being responsible.

3. Have small groups of students create a tableau pose that captures the problem.
4. As a class, have the students create a tableau that captures an *If/Then* that makes the problem bigger.
5. As a class, have students create a tableau that shows captures an *If/Then* that makes the problem smaller.

Homework

SAMPLE RESPONSIBILITY HOMEWORK ACTIVITIES

Subject	Activity	F	S	S	M	T	W	T
Responsibility	Bring back your completed homework by next Friday.							
Problem Scale	Explain the problem scale to three people.							
If/Then Strategies	Explain to the same three people how to write an *If/Then* self-control statement.							
Spelling	Study for _____							
Math	Do 5 minutes of mental math. Multiplication *If I have 2 groups of 2 apples, how many apples do I have?* *If I have 2 groups of 3 apples, how many apples do I have?* *If I have 2 groups of 4 apples, how many apples do I have?*							
Sports	Do at least 20 minutes of exercise.							
Mapping	Draw or write directions to a place you like to go to.							
Manual Skills	Practice tying your shoes.							
Games	Play chess, Monopoly, Uno, Battleship, or a card game.							
Music	Practice an instrument or dance.							
Art	Draw, paint, or create.							
Drama	Write or perform a play, play charades, or role play.							

Sentence Wall: E-mail Home

Salutation

Dear   Mom
         Dad
         Grandma
         Grandpa
         _____

Positive Intro
I hope you are well. I hope you had a good day.

Body

I had a _____ day at school today because I played _____ with my friends.

great	tag
good	man hunt
fabulous	imaginary games
wonderful	on the climbers
tremendous	soccer
fantastic	basketball
phenomenal	chase
remarkable	and talked

I had an _____ day at school today because I _____.

excellent	read
incredible	drew
amazing	learned how to _____
	made a _____
	saw a _____
	learned about _____

Make an *If/Then* statement
If I work hard at school, then _____. If I include all my friends during recess, then _____. If I work quietly during writing, then _____. If I tell a friend that they did a great job, then _____.

Conclusion
I really miss you. I can't wait to see you. xoxo I hope that you have a great day tomorrow. :) Good luck on your _____. Please let me know how your _____ goes.

Sign-off
Love from Sincerely

Pembroke Publishers ©2017 *Keep Growing* by Joey Mandel ISBN 978-1-55138-320-0

4

Independence

Independence

What it is: The ability to start, move through, and finish a task without being told to, and without being helped to accomplish what you can do on your own; trying things on your own, before turning to others to ask for help or for them to do it for you.

What it looks like:

- Not knowing how to do a worksheet, so taking the time to read it over one more time and to look for examples.
- Trying to open something that is hard and working on it for a few minutes without asking someone else to open it for you.
- Sitting down at your desk and starting your work on your own.
- Using the charts and reminders in the classroom to figure out what to do next.
- Looking around to see what other students are doing to figure out what to do next.
- Asking for help on one part of a task you have tried, but cannot do yourself, with the goal of being able to complete the rest of the task on your own.

When a child faces a problem, will they look inward for strategies to solve their problem? Will they look outward to others? Or will they not even attempt to solve it? We want to create children's growth mindsets, the belief that they can solve challenges themselves and that they have the tools to do it.

Examining the child's previous exposure to problem-solving can provide useful information when planning how to explicitly teach independence. When missteps happen, children immediately look for support, looking first to their primary caregivers. If their primary caregivers solve the problems for them and fix each challenge, children start to expect that hard moments will be resolved by someone else. Their mindset becomes more fixed by the experience: *there is a specific way to fix this challenge and it will not be done by me.* This limits a child's ability to move through hard times. Each time there is an obstacle and someone else fixes the problem or tells them what to do, the child loses out on an opportunity to face an uncertainty, to think about what they could do, and to try a few things in order to solve the problem. What is worse, when an adult steps in to do things for a child when it is not needed, it sends a subtle message to the child that they can't do it themselves.

Children are born with predispositions toward fixed or growth mindsets. A fixed mindset is not necessarily the result of a primary caregiver taking over during challenging moments and solving all problems for the child. Yet, as children turn more and more often to their caregivers and teachers for help, the way we respond will either create greater dependence or initiate steps toward independence for the child. If each hard moment is supported by a primary caregiver in a way that allows the child to face unknowns and to try possible resolutions, the child gains confidence in themselves and their ability to figure out and work through challenges. These experiences are what allow children to know that there is uncertainty in the world, that there are hard moments and they can work through them.

Independence in the Classroom

As teachers, every day we think through each activity and consider how it will support practice-based learning. We need to perform a constant triage of information and problem-solving before responding to each student during a challenging moment. What would best serve this student?
- Should the student be encouraged to solve this on their own? What task can I give them that, if they apply themselves, they can accomplish successfully on their own?
- Would the student benefit from social support with peers? What task can I give them that, with peer support, they can accomplish successfully together?
- Should I offer the student support? What task can I give them that, with a little guidance and scaffolding from me, they can accomplish successfully with my indirect support?

The best way for us to respond and help is not constant; it differs from student to student. Since all students have different strengths and struggles, it makes sense that they would benefit by being supported in different ways.

SAMPLE TRIAGE CHARTS

Problem	You Have Noticed about the Student	Student Actions	Teacher Response
A student says to the teacher, "I need a pencil."	• Dependent on others • Weak problem-solving skills	Student asks for help to do something that they should be able to do on their own.	• Independent: Encourage the student to look around the room to find what they are looking for. • Teacher Support: Ask them what they need to do to solve the problem. Stay with them, but do not do anything to get the pencil.

In this Student Response, the student begins solving the problem on their own. But the student is an independent worker whose area of need is positive interaction with others. So the teacher finds a student who could benefit from independence and creates a peer situation in which each child benefits.

Problem	You Have Noticed about Student	Student Response	Task Options
A student drops something and makes a mess.	• Struggles to get along with others • Is very independent	The student begins to clean up on their own.	• Peer Support: Have another student with independent skills help them clean up.

The right kind of teacher response is instrumental in the success a student will find facing a challenge. We can approach each activity and, more specifically, each moment of a challenge or obstacle in the classroom with a quick internal problem-solving model: consider what the challenge is and how we can support the student to overcome that challenge in a way that is best for them. In this way, we are constantly setting up students for successful experiences in facing a challenge and overcoming it, no matter how big or small the challenge might be. The way we respond to students develops their mindset and their ability to face bigger harder challenges in the future.

If we take that opportunity away from our students, quickly telling them what to do, doing it for them, or setting challenges that are too hard for them to succeed with, then we take away their opportunity to successfully experience trying or doing something hard. If we understand our role in the classroom to be facilitators of students doing things for themselves, thinking for themselves, and problem-solving for themselves, then we will more often give them those important moments to practice their skills.

Children who were raised in controlling homes did not do as well on the Marshmallow Test (see page 10). They had fewer distracting strategies to help them successfully delay the reward. If we do not give children ownership over their lives, then they lack chances to make their own decisions and to practice self-control.

A Practice-Based Learning Environment for Independence

1. Support students in believing that there is value in attempting challenges on their own, even if they do not accomplish the goal.
2. Have students develop *If/Then* strategies that focus on ways of solving problems on their own.
3. Step back while students approach and struggle with challenges; allow them space to execute their *If/Then* strategies even if the task or goal is not achieved.

Strategies and Activities

Oral Language: Sharing Circle

1. Prompt students by asking them to reflect on what they do independently.
   • Ask students to share or list activities that they do on their own.
   • Ask students to share or list activities that they think a student in the next higher grade could do on their own.
   • Ask students to share or list activities that they do on their own, but that a student in the next lower grade could likely not do on their own.
   • Ask students to share or list activities that they think a student much older could do on their own. Give examples, using names of students in higher grades.

2. Ask: *What do you do when you need to...* List actions that most children in the class do independently, for example:
   - Blow your nose
   - Sharpen your pencil
   - Change your shoes
   - Get a drink of water

   Ask what the classroom would look like if every child asked for help for these actions. Ask: *What are some other things in our class that we tend to ask for help for, but that we could maybe try to be more independent in doing?*
3. Instruct students:

   Close your eyes. Imagine there is a really cool box in the classroom. It is covered with your favorite patterns and has stickers on it of some of the things that you love. You walk over to the box. The box is closed. It does not have a lock on is, but the lid seems stuck. What is the first thing you do?

4. Possible responses include
   - I ask for help.
   - I look around to see if there is something I could use to open the box.
   - I keep trying to open it.

5. Negative responses to the challenge include
   - I would give up.
   - I would walk away and find something else to do.
   - I would cry.
   - I would complain that this is too hard.

   Since you have set up the problem as a preferred task, one that students are motivated to solve, they are less likely to respond with negative answers. Point out that we sometimes have negative responses to problems in life, but they tend to come when we are faced with tasks that we do not like to do. The fact that the box is cool, that students want to know what is in it, gives them the natural motivation to try hard to do something that is not doable right away. Ask students: *If we responded in positive ways to a non-preferred task, would our life be easier or harder?*
6. Ask students to step into the circle if they agree with the statement.
   - If I think before I ask for help, then I might come up with the answer on my own.
   - If I look around the room to see what other students are doing, then I might figure out what I should do.
   - If I look at the examples on the board, then I will figure out what I can do next.
   - If I ask a friend for help, then they will help me.
   - If I think for a moment, then I will probably come up with a way to solve my problem myself.

Reading: Book Club

Support students in understanding the exact behavior that needs to occur so that they can work in independent groups, reading together. Explicitly outlining task expectations is essential. It is hard for some students to be independent without clear goals and steps to follow. It is hard for them to take risks and guess what they might be able to do. They worry that they might make the wrong choice. As the year evolves, keep encouraging students to make decisions on their own and to problem-solve the unknown. In order for them to do this, they need a base structure of what they should and should not do. Then we can encourage them to make choices on their own, based on the understood expectations.

1. Have book club groups make reminder schedules or lists to remind them about their jobs.

   Sample Book Club Schedule
   1. Read one book from the red bin.
   2. Read one book from the blue bin.
   3. Read a poem together.
   4. Comment on what the text reminded you of.
   Tip: While sharing, use a connection sign instead of interrupting your friend.

2. Explain that there will be lots of little bumps along the way in book club that they will not know exactly how to solve right away. And since you are busy reading with one group, you will not be able to come over and solve all of their problems. Go over with students different ways that they could solve the challenges that will arise during book club. Ask:
   • Do your actions let you keep working?
   • Does your *If/Then* statement result in you doing nothing or continuing your work?

3. Place a problem scale on the table. Ask each student to write on a lightning bolt one challenge they think might occur during book club; e.g., *We finish the book and finish talking about it before the period is over.* Have them place their lightning bolts on the problem scale.
4. Discuss with them thoughts they might have that would not solve their problem; e.g., *I don't know what to do; I need someone to tell me what to do next.* Give each student a speech bubble and have them write on it what they would say or ask if they thought that way; e.g. "Teacher, what should I do next?" Ask them if they think they want to try to solve problems on their own first, before asking for help.
5. Have students use this problem to make an *If/Then* statement that can be left at the table when you are working with another group:

   If we finish our work early, *then* we can think of one more thing to talk about that happened in the book.
   If we finish our work early, *then* we can pick our book for tomorrow.
   If we finish our work early, *then* we can make a chart to show what we know.
   If we finish our work early, *then* we can finish other class work we have not completed.

6. During book club, if students ask your for help, instead of ignoring them or helping them, ask them to review their *If/Then* chart and see if they can use it to try to solve their problem.

7. After book club, review new challenges that have come up and brainstorm more *If/Then* statements they could use for the next book club.

Writing: Weekly Letter Home

We can expand our students' writing to include communication home to their parents. Students are responsible for an accurate reflection of the week. We need to give them the tools for independent communication between home and school. Weekly letters home have a tremendous capability to shift fixed mindsets. Some students struggle to begin and continue writing. They can't put pen to paper; if they come to a word they can't spell, they stop, freeze, and are unable to continue until you tell them how to spell the word. Weekly letter writing using a familiar writing form, repeating the recount throughout the year, supports practice-based learning with the support of the teacher and their parents at home.

See page 53 for a template for the weekly letters home. I photocopy the weekly homework checklist on the back of the letters home.

1. At the end of each week, have students write a letter home to their parents detailing events of the week. This task serves many functions: it provides parents and teachers with a weekly sample of a child's writing from the beginning to the end of the year; it takes the responsibility for communication of classroom activities off the teacher and places it with students; it gives weekly voice to students to reflect and share strengths and struggles.

Letter Templates

It is important to create your own letter templates, both for your class and for individual students. Templates need to tailor the writing page for students and their needs as writers. Some students write just a few sentences; some write many. Some students have huge handwriting; others use tiny letters. Offering them a different writing page makes sure they are always striving to compete a sheet of paper that is at their level. If a child has tiny handwriting and writes just a few sentences, the right page structure allows their page to look as complete as that of a student with large handwriting.

There are many ways to tweak a page so that it fits the needs of each student; for example, having a large box at the top of the page for correcting misspelled words or for a student's own sentence walls will allow each student's final product to appear complete. Make a variety of letter pages and help students identify which template is best for them. If students choose a template different from the one at their level, help them assess the template and pick the one that is best for them. If they have chosen and begun, help them see it as an opportunity for them to consider how much effort and thought they put into looking at and choosing from the templates. Over time, you can shift formats as a student grows in their writing ability, writes more, and gains more control over their handwriting.

On page 49, I have provided Sample Writing Checklists to place at the bottom of the letter template. Whether graphic or in writing, they need to match students' reading levels. The visual checklist is appropriate for lower reading levels; text checklists can be used with more advanced students.

SAMPLE WRITING CHECKLISTS

On the line _____	Capital A	Period. .	New ideas	Add details	Look it over.

GOAL	I DID IT!
My writing is on the line and neat.	
My first letters have capitals.	
My sentences end with periods.	
My letter formation is correct (not backwards).	
I give details about things that happened at school.	
I use the word "because" to explain my statements.	

See page 36 for more on sentence walls.

2. Students can use the Sentence Wall: Weekly Recount on page 54 to support their writing.

Media Studies: Independence Poster

Just as I do when I am determining how to support a child, I always use one-on-one teacher time as the last choice in my decision-making triage. I encourage a process in which getting teacher help is their last action. They try to solve the problem themselves, then with the help of others, before asking for teacher support.

1. Review the Oral Language circle on independence (see page 45).
2. Make posters with students that detail exact behaviors that promote independence: *if* they do them, *then* they will be able to solve problems on their own.
3. Review these posters and previously made ones. Refer to rubrics while reviewing student-made posters in the classroom.
4. Review the main goal to ensure students understand the message they will be promoting.
5. Have students work in small groups to determine the goal and ways to communicate the message on their own.
6. Offer various graphic organizers or starting points, so they have a way to chunk the information.
7. Write key words on the board with them as they brainstorm steps to independence.

I like to begin by making suggestions that make students consider what *not* to do. For example, I write that whenever they have a problem in class, the first thing they should do is run up and ask the teacher.

Date: _____ Name: _____

When I do not know what to do, there are things that I can try to do.

THINK FIRST:
If I think about ways that I could try myself, then I might come up with a new idea of my own.
If I try a few things, then one of them might may work.

LOOK SECOND:
If I look around to see if there are examples, then I might figure out the step that I am missing.
If I look around the room, then I will get clues.
If I look around, then I might see what other people are doing.

ASK THIRD:
If I ask a friend for help, then someone will give me a strategy, but not do it for me.
If I ask a teacher for help, then they will give me a hint, but not tell me what to do.

If we solve problems on our own, then we will _____.

Math: Response to a Challenge

Have students self-reflect about their independent response to non-preferred task.

1. Begin by helping students consider which questions would allow them to establish their independent actions when faced with a challenge.
2. List possible If/Then statements that explore which actions students could take when things get hard. Use these statements to design a questionnaire for your class.

Sample Questionnaire

Check the box if you agree with this statement.
- ☐ If it is hard, then I still begin the task.
- ☐ If it is hard, then I ask the teacher for help.
- ☐ If it is hard, then I refuse to even start the task.
- ☐ If it is hard, then I rush through it and finish it quickly just to be done.
- ☐ If it is hard, then I try to make my work better.
- ☐ If it is hard, then I can look around to see who can help me.
- ☐ If it is hard, then I look at a friend's sheet and copy their answers.
- ☐ If it is hard, then I try to figure out one thing I can do on my own.
- ☐ If it is hard, then I read the questions again.

Art/Drama: Independent Imagination

1. Tell students to close their eyes. Present students with a problem:

   Imagine that you are in your room by yourself. You want to play with a puzzle, but it is on a high shelf. What do you think? How do you feel? What do you do? Do you give up and walk away? Do you call for your parents? Do you try to get the puzzle? Do you find another toy? Do you call for your parents to get it down for you? Imagine that your parents are not available to help you. Let's examine what you are thinking and how you feel.

2. Remind them to keep their eyes closed. Have them imagine feeling defeated:

   Imagine what your face looks like as you are looking at the puzzle, way up high, that puzzle that you can't reach. Are your eyes sad? Are you crying? Is your lip quivering? What happens to your body? Do your shoulders slump? Does your head fall? Do you fall to the ground? Do you flop on your bed? Do you leave your room? Are you sad that the puzzle is high, out of your reach?
   What are you thinking? Maybe you are thinking, This is hopeless, I could never get this puzzle, it is just too high. I will never play with it again.

Different thoughts elicit different emotions. Thoughts about being defeated, alone, or helpless often bring about sad feelings. Thoughts about self-righteousness, fault, and blame often bring about angry feelings. Thoughts about judgment by others, expectation, and personal weaknesses often bring about feelings of anxiety.

3. Have them imagine anger:

   Or when you see that puzzle, do your eyes scrunch up? Do you stare at the puzzle with a fixed glare? Does your head shake? Does a deep hot feeling go up your whole body? Are your shoulders tight? Do you plant your feet into the ground so hard they could push through the floor?
   If so, what are you thinking? Maybe you are thinking Who put that puzzle up so high that I could not get it? Why do things like this always happen to me? Why is everyone against me?
   What could you think to yourself that might help you try to figure out a way to get that puzzle down?

4. Using their imagined anger, prompt students to work up an *If/Then* statement:

   If you blame it on someone else, then…

5. Have students imagine a positive response:

   Or when you see the puzzle high up on the shelf, do you see this as a challenge you can face? Do you see it as a chance for you to figure out how you will get that puzzle down all by yourself? What do you do? How do you get it?

6. Using their imagined response, prompt students to work up an *If/Then* statement:

   If you keep trying to get it on your own, then…

Homework

Subject	Activity	F	S	S	M	T	W	T
Independence	• Take your homework out of your bag on your own • Find a good location at home where you can post your homework checklist and check in with it everyday • Set homework goals before the week starts (highlight the boxes to indicate which activities you plan to do over the week) • Check off the boxes and follow up with incomplete homework yourself							
Problem Scale	Make a problem scale that details something you have been asking for help on but think you could begin to try to do on your own.							
If/Then	Write an *If/Then* self-control statement that will help you practice working independently.							
Spelling	• Learn how to give yourself a spelling test • Look over your own work and make your corrections							
Writing	Weekly Letter Home Have parents show how to begin to edit your own work, so that you can be more independent. *At home, with a helper, I am working on* _____							
Math	• Learn to occupy your brain while waiting. • Slowly build knowledge by starting with something easy, then increasing the difficulty.							
Sports	• Practice your favorite sport by yourself • Identify one part of your game you need to work on, and find a way to work on it on your own at home *If I am a slow runner, then it will affect my baseball game, so I can practice running sprints.* *If I have a weak shot in hockey, then I could do push-ups each night.*							
Board Games	• When playing games with your family, choose the game and set it up • When people are too busy to play with you, find fun games that you can play on your own, like cards							
Chores	• Pick three jobs around the house that your parents are having trouble doing and do them without being asked							

Letter Template

DATE _____

_____

_____

_____

_____

To _____

_____

_____

_____

_____

From _____

Sentence Wall: Weekly Recount

Salutation

Dear   Mom
        Dad
        Grandma
        Grandpa
        _____

Introduction

I had a _____ week at school because _____.
        great
        good
        fabulous
        wonderful
        fantastic
        remarkable
        hard
        difficult

Body

This week at school, we have been learning _____ in _____.
                    rhymes   language class
                    to write numbers   math class
                    typing   computer time
                    the B note   music class
                    equations   math class
                    to walk safely   the halls

I _____ because_____.
  loved it   I have never done that before
  liked it   we were all laughing
  thought it was great   I learned how to do something new
  did not like it   I already know how to do it
  thought it was hard   I could not figure out how to do it

At recess I have been playing _____ with _____.
                    tag   lots of different friends.
                    man hunt
                    imaginary games
                    on the climbers
                    soccer
                    basketball
                    chase

Pembroke Publishers ©2017 *Keep Growing* by Joey Mandel ISBN 978-1-55138-320-0

Sentence Wall: Weekly Recount cont'd.

I _____ because _____.

had fun with them	I have never done that before
was upset	it was confusing and hard to do
loved it	I learned how to do something new
think I need a break	it is my favorite time of the day
wish it could always be recess	I could not figure out how to do it

Conclusion

I had a _____ week, I hope that next week we can _____.

great	learn even more about maps
good	do more work!
fabulous	play more music on the _____
wonderful	have more time to _____
tricky	spend more time on _____
fantastic	listen to more lessons on about_____
challenging	
remarkable	
hard	

Pembroke Publishers ©2017 *Keep Growing* by Joey Mandel ISBN 978-1-55138-320-0

5

Self-Regulation

> **Self-Regulation**
>
> What it is: The ability of the body and mind to be ready to learn. When a child is self-regulated their internal energy level is calm and alert: not overstimulated or so excited, overwhelmed, jumpy, or charged that they are bouncing around, unable to sit and process learning; not understimulated or so sluggish, tired, or distant that they cannot actively learn.
>
> What it looks like:
> - Sitting up in a desk, turned toward the person who is talking
> - Listening to another person talk and hearing the words that they say
> - Playing a game (like tag) with others and controlling the body's movements
> - Being able to read and understand the words that are on a page

There are self-regulation programs that use kid-friendly language to break down for students what makes their bodies move and think fast and what helps slow this down. Check out The Alert Program, Zones of Regulation, or Stop Now And Plan.

When facing problems, some children quickly lose control of themselves and become dysregulated; they cannot think and they lack full control over their bodies. A calm mind is essential to thinking rationally and realistically. When overstimulation, upset, or stress causes someone to be dysregulated, they are unable to think clearly or use self-talk strategies to apply growth-mindset thinking to even small problems. A calm body is essential to maintaining self-control and utilizing effective strategies that support reasoned responses. When someone is dysregulated, they are unable to apply self-control strategies to take a step away, to take a breath or, to wait their turn. It is growth-mindset thinking that prevents challenging problems from upsetting a child to the point of becoming dysregulated; therefore, those with growth mindsets will become upset less often in life. They interpret challenges as less threatening because they do not have core beliefs that assume that the problem is all about them or that someone or something is acting against them. So with a growth mindset, the interpretation of the event is less stressful.

Self-Regulation in the Classroom

We are always telling children to calm down, to slow down, and to pay attention. These requests are the essence of asking children to self-regulate. Most report cards ask teachers to evaluate self-regulation, so we need to ensure that we have success criteria that allow students and ourselves move from self-regulation expectations to a self-regulation teaching plan.

Smooth transitions are all about self-regulation. How do we move students from running and yelling outside to quietly walking upstairs after recess? How do we excite and laugh with students one minute and then help them maintain control for the next activity? For example, silent reading right after lunch recess can be used as a self-regulation tool. Teach students how to link the impact the reading has on their bodies: *When I come in from recess, my body feels out of control. If I read for twenty minutes, then my body will feel softer and ready to learn.*

A Practice-Based Learning Environment for Self-Regulation

1. Support students in identifying their energy level in a non-judgmental way.
2. Let students assess a hard moment and make their own *If/Then* statements that will make the problem smaller.
3. If students make mistakes, give them an opportunity to try again using their *If/Then* statements to make the problem smaller.

Strategies and Activities

Oral Language: Coming Into the Circle

1. Ask the students to come to the circle, then go to another end of the room and sit down. Do not do anything; do not tell the students again to come to the circle. Observe what happens. Some students will not come to the circle; most will go off and play. Some will look at you, confused.
2. After a while, go to the circle and ask students to come again, without demands and without asking students individually. Without direct teacher instructions, it takes students a very long time to come to the circle; once there, they sit and talk and play.
3. Have students reflect on their self-regulation. What was their behavior like without the teacher telling them many times what was expected, without repeated requests or warnings?
4. Reflect on the kind of classroom everyone wants. Do they want a classroom with independent students, responsible for themselves without the teacher managing them? Explain that wanting it is the easy part. Discuss how self-regulation is the key to this ability because students have to make decisions to stop doing the fun things; they will need to stop playing, stop talking with friends. With a growth mindset, open classroom discussions about what works and what helps you as a class become instrumental in providing the tools for self-regulation.
5. Explore with students how, as a teacher, you typically get students to come to the circle and the work you need to do to bring everyone in quietly. Once some students are in the circle, they wait for so long that they being playing and talking too. Ask them which activities you could do as a class while they wait for students to come to the carpet.

Counting in a Circle

In my class there is a number line on the carpet. Students who are waiting for other students begin counting together backwards from 100, and ensure that we are forming a round circle on the carpet. This seems simple, but without direct repetitive support some students have a hard time knowing where their body should be as part of the group. They might sit inside the circle or with their back to everyone. Those who struggle to count with others need to learn to join their voices with others while sharing space. Our routine explicitly shapes the circle and sets it up for success. When we begin this activity in September, children scream out the numbers. With direct support, they learn to slowly chant the numbers, decreasing in volume. By the time they are at 10, I can hardly hear most students; as the final students come to the carpet, the larger group is whispering the final numbers of the countdown. Each day I explain to students that this is self-regulation: we get our moving bodies calm and we enter a new space, alert and ready to learn.

---

6. Have students step into the circle if they agree with these statements:
   - *Your body sometimes feels fast and energetic.*
   - *Your body sometimes moves quickly and you can't slow it down.*
   - *You sometimes wish you could slow yourself down.*

7. Go around the circle and ask students to list techniques that could be used in class to wait for others to come.

   - Count backward inside your head.
   - Tell yourself a story inside your head as you wait.
   - Think of four things that make you happy.

8. Prompt students for more techniques: "If your body moves a lot and it is hard for you to sit on the carpet and listen to lessons, do you think it would help if you did 10 push-ups before you got to the carpet?"
9. Have students turn to the one closest to them and make an *If/Then* statement they think might work for them. Possible answers:

   - *If* I sit and look at the maps, *then* I will be slowing my body while I wait.
   - *If* I sit and count backward inside my head, *then* I will be slowing my body while I wait.
   - *If* I do push-ups just before I come to the circle, *then* I will get some of the energy out of my body before I come to the circle.
   - *If* I sit and think about my favorite toy, *then* I will put myself in a positive mood while I wait.

Reading: Silent Reading

Students often come into the classroom in physical states that are not conducive to learning. Students can lack energy, looking like they want to sleep, they can be tired, hungry, sad, or lethargic. Or they can enter full of energy, unable to sit still, stop talking or moving; they could be agitated or angry. Classroom routines like these have structure but give students choice promote self-regulation:

- Sit on a chair or in the circle for a lesson.
- Sit at one table group during silent reading, but another table group for math.
- Walk through the halls quietly; speak in a whisper to your partner beside you.

Self-Regulation Programs

The Zones of Regulation and the Alert Program are self-regulation programs. In the four Zones of Regulation the Blue Zone and Red Zone are deregulated states: in the Blue Zone one's body is sluggish and/or tired and one might feel sad; in the Red Zone one's body is hyper and/or out of control and one might feel angry. The Yellow Zone is a warning zone in which one can still make choices to self-regulate; one might feel frustrated or worried. The Green Zone is the regulated state the program helps children to achieve, when one's body is calm, yet alert, when one feels good and ready to learn.

The Alert Program compares the body to an engine. If the child is calm and alert, the child's engine is said to be running Just Right; this is equivalent to the Green Zone. If the child's engine is running too slowly, it is Too Low; this is equivalent to the Blue Zone. If the child's engine is running too fast and out of control, it is Too High; this is equivalent to the Red Zone.

This process can be self-regulating for you as a teacher, as it provides thirty minutes a day to target students' needs. After a month of scaffolding and slow development, the system can operate without the teacher, and offers students daily time to work on important development that might not be a part of the yearly curriculum.

Silent reading is one of those routines that acts as a physical regulator. Silent reading is, in and of itself, self-regulating for most students. First thing in the morning or after lunch, you can use a long silent reading period to fit the needs of all students and yourself.

1. Set up the quiet reading environment. You will be using a variety of activities, focused on individual needs and quiet reading.
2. Know your students. Chart information about your students' energy and alertness levels. For example, students who come in from recess with Zone and Alert levels of Red and Too High could benefit from self-calming activities to help them transition back into the classroom; a lethargic student who has Zone and Alert levels of Blue or Too Low could benefit from activities that would help make them more alert. Green or Just Right would signal that the child is often in a state in which they are ready to learn and is able to transition from active at recess to calm in class.

I would identify ESL learners and students on the Autism Spectrum who struggle to chat with others as having Social Communication needs. I would identify a student with Fine Motor needs if their writing is messy, and Gross Motor needs if they struggle during gym class.

Include on the chart students' academic needs—e.g., Reading, Math, Motor Skills, Social Communication—to plan silent reading time. Review games and activities and set up practice centres that support each students' energy and alertness levels as well as their learning needs. For example, a student with Math needs could be partnered with another student on a simple and fun math activity; a student with Reading needs could be partnered with two other students to read a hi-lo book; a student charted at Green and Just Right levels could sometimes be partnered with another student to play a game during silent reading, or could do a cutting-and-drawing activity if they have Fine Motor needs; a student at Red and Too High levels could do silent reading alone; a student at Blue and Too Low levels could be partnered with other students with learning needs. Note you can schedule different activities for silent reading on different days to meet all of a student's needs. See sample chart below.

SAMPLE READING SCHEDULE FOR INDIVIDUAL STUDENTS

Student	Zone/Alert Level	Academic Needs	Monday Task	Tuesday Task	Wednesday Task	Thursday Task	Friday Task
Annie	Green Just Right	Reading	Read to a younger student	Silent Reading	Read to a younger student	Silent Reading	Read to a younger student
Tyler	Red Too High	Math	Partner with Sam on a fun and simple math activity	Partner with Sam on a fun and simple math activity	Partner with Sam on a fun and simple math activity	Partner with Sam on a fun and simple math activity	Partner with Sam on a fun and simple math activity
Ben	Blue Too Low	None	Partner with Social Communication student to play Barrier Game	Partner with Math group to help teach math	Silent Reading	Partner with Math group to help teach math	Partner with Emily to play Barrier Game

In the Barrier Game, two students work together to communicate a message to each other, using language only. They sit across from each other with their view of each other obstructed and holding the same task; e.g., a maze or coloring sheet. One student explains verbally what the other needs to do. See *Moment to Moment* (Mandel, 2013) for more game ideas.

If a student says they love silent reading, then you can have them do another activity daily for 20–25 minutes and end with 5–10 minutes of silent reading; alternatively, they can do the other activity three days a week and still have plenty of silent reading time.

3. Once silent reading has worked well for two weeks or more, let students know that you will be beginning centres for different quiet activities during silent reading. The centres will offer them time to work on something that makes sense for them. Just like the homework program that focuses on areas of need, silent reading classroom time will be used strategically to allow all students time to read. It will also allow all students time to work independently or with someone on things that are harder for them, for which we want to set aside time to practice and improve.

4. Begin to pull students into the hall or a quiet area of the classroom and explain options for them during silent reading. Silent reading is a time in the day that has two goals: to practice reading; also to help us get our bodies ready to learn for the rest of the afternoon. Ask: *Do you think silent reading is working for you? Do you think you are reading during all of the silent reading time, some of it, or none of it? Do you think there are other things in school we might want to use some of silent reading time to work on?*

5. Have the student fill out a short survey:

Do I like silent reading?	Yes ___ No ___
Do I need to work on my reading?	Yes ___ No ___
Is there other school work that is harder for me than reading?	Yes ___ No ___
Could I use my silent reading time to work on that?	Yes ___ No ___

Using the information, help the student create a schedule that details their weekly activities and lists their goals.

For a math activity, ask the teacher of a class two to three years below your grade for the game they have found is most fun for students.

SAMPLE SCHEDULE

Monday	Tuesday	Wednesday	Thursday	Friday
Go to the round table at the back of the room. Work with Devante on math.	Silent reading	Go to the long table in the hallway. Play Barrier Game with Summer.	Silent reading	Go to the round table at the back of the room. Work with Devante on math.

6. Pick simple activities to start with. Begin slowly, starting with one group of students at a time. Do not begin with another group until the first working group is able to set up and work independently. Keep students in the same groups for a few days.

Writing: E-mail the Teacher

When children are dysregulated, especially emotionally, they often face problems at school. They go home and begin to reflect on these problems without the personal tools to help calm themselves down, and with parents who, only hearing one side of the story, can often themselves get upset. If a student has had a hard day at school, have them consider sending an e-mail to you. The goal of the e-mails is to take an honest look at the problem that occurred during the day and to reflect on it. The student can explain the challenge and detail what they need; they also can take ownership of their actions and make a plan for next time. This process does not focus on mistakes and does not seek to punish students for missteps made. It attempts to examine daily challenges as the learning experience.

1. Have the student level the problem using the problem scale and explain the problem from their viewpoint. They can also list what they wish they had not done and explore strategies that they could have used to make the problem smaller. See page 65 for The Problem I Had Today template.
2. Send students home with sentence walls to help them reflect on the problem and then set self-regulation goals. See Sentence Wall for Self-Advocacy E-mail on page 66.
3. Students complete checklists that ensure that they have proofread their work and added detail; it is effective to include checklists that have them reflect on the content and validity of their perspective. Encourage students to read each question one at a time and to answer them honestly. Consider modelling self-talk with them: "Hmm. Let me see. Is my e-mail polite? I obviously want to check *Yes* right away. But first I need to make sure that the e-mail does not use harsh words to tell someone what they did wrong or what I am mad about. I need to read over my e-mail in order to make sure it is polite."

Media Studies: Intended Message

Use this activity to explain self-regulation to students and show images of the benefits of being regulated.

1. Examine the message intended for Self-Regulation. Gather self-regulation resources you have at school. Gather as many images as you can: look for images on relaxation or mindfulness CDs, mediation books, flyers.
2. Place the materials in the middle of your circle or on a table. Invite students to look at the products.
3. Ask students to try to figure out what message that is being put across. What feelings are the books and CDs trying to get you to feel? What are the manufacturers of the products trying to convince people that their product will do?
4. Ask students for key words and make a list: e.g., *calm, relaxed, soft, sleepy, safe, slow.*

Math: Calming Surveys

Students can create surveys that determine the best strategy to calm their bodies.

Primary

1. Have students come up with one self-regulation question and two to three responses for others to choose from:

   What can I do when my body keeps moving when I'm on the carpet?
   When my body moves on the carpet, I prefer to do a lot of push-ups or count quietly in my head to slow my body down.

2. Students turn this question into a survey to give their classmates.

SAMPLE SURVEY

When my body moves when I am in circle, I can:	
Do pushups.	Count quietly in my head

3. Explain that each day we make choices that help support our self-regulation. What works for some people does not work for others. It is important to reflect on what works best for each of us as individuals.
4. As a class, review the individual data on which strategies work best for each student. Have each student review and reflect on the strategies that help them and those that help their friends. As a class, chart the data.

Junior

1. Have students take the Management Quiz provided on page 67.
2. Once they complete the quiz, have them analyze their own results. Students can track their answers to gather information about their thinking patterns.
3. Once Junior students have taken a few self-regulation surveys, challenge them to make up their own survey that examines the way they respond to different problems and what they can do to help them respond in a better way.

Art/Drama: Re-enacting the Marshmallow Test

1. Describe the Marshmallow Test and its results to students; see page 10.
2. Ask: *If you were given the choice, would you want one marshmallow right away or would you wait for two?*

> In the test, most children said that they wanted two marshmallows; they said they would wait and have both marshmallows. However, many were not able to wait and at some point ate the first marshmallow. This tells us that the children were motivated by the marshmallow and wanted it, but were not able to wait long enough to earn the second marshmallow.

3. Put a marshmallow or toy in the middle of the carpet or on the desk. Ask students to imagine a child in the room alone. Ask students to imagine what the child might look like, waiting in a room with a marshmallow. Students might tell you the child is

   - staring at the marshmallow
   - going near the marshmallow
   - trying to smell the marshmallow
   - touching the marshmallow

4. Ask students how well a child might do waiting for the marshmallow if they gazed at it, stared at it, tried to touch it, tried to lick it. The students will likely understand that those who behave this way would have a harder time waiting for the second marshmallow. They know that thinking about it and looking at it would make it harder to resist the marshmallow in front of them.

5. Ask students to consider a child who is able to wait for the second one, who "passes the test." What might that child look like? What might that child do? They might tell you the child is

   - looking away
   - turning away
   - closing their eyes
   - singing a song in their head

6. Discuss with students how those tricks would help the child. Ask if they can think of other things the child might say to themselves or think inside their head. Answers you might receive:

- *I can do it.*
- *It will be better to have two.*
- *I have to wait for dessert all the time. I know I can do this.*
- *If I pretend the marshmallow is a cloud, it might not seem so tasty.*

7. Explain to students that it was not that some children wanted two marshmallows while others wanted one, but that some children were able to wait for a certain amount of time to earn that second marshmallow. These children had strategies to help them get what they wanted; they were able to distract themselves in order to be able to resist something they wanted. Ask students if this test can be applied to anything else in their life, home, or classroom. How could it help them create their own *If/Then* statements that list what they have to do and then what they get to do? Possible *If/Then* pairings:

   Math, then recess
   Set the table, then eat
   Dinner, then dessert
   Reading, then snack
   Homework, then TV

Homework

SAMPLE SELF-REGULATION HOMEWORK ACTIVITIES

Subject	Activity	F	S	S	M	T	W	T
Problem Scale	Make a problem scale for an activity during which you notice your body moves around a lot or you become upset or sad.							
If/Then	Write an *If/Then* self-control statement that reminds you to use a strategy to help you sit through something hard or boring.							
Spelling	• Sit down and work on something that is hard. • Experience the frustration of not knowing something, then work on it until you get it.							
Math	• Learn to occupy your brain while waiting. • Slowly build knowledge by starting with something easy, then increasing the difficulty.							
Sports	• During sports, go from moving quickly to stopping. • While moving quickly do something that requires precision.							
Board Games	While playing board games • wait for your turn. • resist the urge to touch everyone's piece. • stay in the social space that the game is taking place in. • resist the urge to grab things from friends.							
Chores	• Start a job you do not want to do. • Continue working even if you want to stop.							

The Problem I Had Today

Problem

	No	Small	Medium	Large	Huge

0_____5_____ 10

At the time it happened, this felt like a _____ problem.
Now it feels like a _____ problem.
If I have a controlled response, I think I can/can't turn this into a small problem.

Reaction I had that made the problem BIGGER.
I wish I had not
☐ yelled at my friend.
☐ talked over my friend.
☐ fooled around in the hall.
☐ hit my friend.
☐ walked out of the classroom.
☐ run away.
☐ _____.
☐ _____.

Response I can make to make the problem SMALLER next time.
Next time I will try to
☐ let other students have their turns too.
☐ take a break before I get so upset.
☐ sit more quietly so that I am not disrupting the learning of others.
☐ stop talking while you are speaking so that I can hear what you need.
☐ take a deep breath, close my eyes, and think first, before I act.
☐ go get a quick drink of water in the hall to calm myself down.
☐ do a few push-ups and stretches.
☐ think of something that makes me happy.
☐ _____.
☐ _____.

IF/THEN
If I _____
_____, then _____
_____

 I wonder if next time you could
☐ give me one more chance.
☐ tell me exactly what you need me to do.
☐ understand that I am trying my best.
☐ listen to my side of the story too.
☐ use our signal to remind me to slow down and breathe.
☐ help me by _____.
☐ let me _____.
☐ remind me to try to _____.
☐ _____

Pembroke Publishers ©2017 *Keep Growing* by Joey Mandel ISBN 978-1-55138-320-0

Sentence Wall for Self-Advocacy E-mail

Salutation
Dear _____   Teacher

Positive Intro
I hope you are well. I can't wait to see you. Did you have a nice day?

My favorite part of the day was when I/we _____.

           read stories
           read during silent reading
           read a book outside
           sang songs
           wrote a story
           played football
           played soccer
           played tag
           learned something new
           ate an amazing _____

I _____ it because _____.

loved	it was something I have never done before
liked	we all got along
appreciated	it was exciting
enjoyed	it was new
	it was relaxing
	it was delicious

Body of the Message

I had a _____ day at school today because I _____.

hard	got hurt when _____
sad	felt nervous when _____
tricky	did not understand _____
miserable	was left out of _____
challenging	could not figure out how to _____
difficult	got in trouble for _____
	had a fight with _____
	was hurt by _____

I felt _____ because someone _____.

mad	did not let me _____
sad	told me to _____
jealous	let other kids _____
embarrassed	said that _____
nervous	made me _____

Pembroke Publishers ©2017 *Keep Growing* by Joey Mandel ISBN 978-1-55138-320-0

Management Quiz

1. You are upset because you were tobogganing down the hill and a kid banged into you. What do you do to calm yourself? A) Close your eyes and count to 10. B) Remind yourself that the kid must not have meant to do it. C) Nothing; there is nothing that you can do to help calm yourself.

2. If your teacher tells you that you can't play a game you want to play, what will likely calm you down? A) Looking up at the sky. B) Telling yourself that the teacher has the right to set rules. C) Nothing; there is nothing that can help you calm down from a problem like this.

3. Your friend invites other people over, but not you. Would you be more likely to help yourself feel better by A) going to a private space and doing a bunch of jumping jacks and push-ups, B) telling yourself that they often invite you over and this time, they are simply going to spend time with someone else, or C) doing nothing, because you know that this is a level 10 problem and that nothing can make you feel better?

4. Your parents tell you to turn off the TV. Would it help you to A) go outside and play a game? B) put some music on? C) throw a huge tantrum and melt down?

5. You are working on a group project and your partner either does nothing at all or starts to take over and make all the decisions. In order to stay calm and keep working, it would be best for you to A) get a fidget and squeeze it really hard the whole time you are working with her? B) tell yourself that this student has issues of their own; she works on being flexible while you work on keeping calm? C) give up, because this type scenario sends you over the edge every time?

6. You run a great race and win, but the referee disqualifies you for a false start. In order to keep your cool, you A) take long slow deep breaths. B) turn away from the referee and tell yourself that you will do better next time. C) can't do anything to stay cool in a situation like this one.

7. Your classroom is really noisy today, something that often makes you upset. Before you get upset, the best strategy for you to use would be A) going for a walk in the hall. B) humming a soft tune in your head to block out the loud noises. C) none; once the noise is in your head, it will never get out.

8. The summer is about to start and you have nothing to do. Your parents tell you that you need to make a plan so that you will be happy. Would you rather A) get a hobby and play games? B) you use the time to just sit, relax, and think? C) nothing; the summer is going to be miserable no matter what?

9. You have a major test coming up in class and are beginning to feel panicky. You can help yourself feel better A) by getting yourself a drink. B) by repeating to yourself "I can do this, it will be fine." C) in no way; you always fail tests because you have panic attacks and this is something that will never change.

10. Your teacher just singled you out in front of the class for not doing your homework. She says that you better shape up, or she will call your parents. In order to console yourself, you A) smile at her and nod, then do a few little body stretches to shake out the tension in your body. B) tell yourself that everyone gets called out by teachers now and then and it is okay. C) can't do anything; this type of problem is so significant that it is impossible to console yourself.

Pembroke Publishers ©2017 *Keep Growing* by Joey Mandel ISBN 978-1-55138-320-0

6

Perspective

What it is: The ability to think about and consider the thoughts and needs of others; the ability to consider a problem from another person's point of view. It is the understanding that people feel differently about problems because everyone reacts to situations, problems, and experiences in varying ways.

What it looks like:

- Being able to express a problem from another's point of view.
- Understanding why an adult lets other students go first.
- Giving someone else more than what is fair because you know the other person needs it.
- Apologizing because you can consider how the other person might have felt because of your behavior.
- Being physically aware of other students in the room, sharing space and moving around people and out of their way.

As children begin to understand that other people also have thoughts and feelings about each event around them, it helps them understand different sides to the story.

When a child faces a daily problem, their interpretation of the problem and their ability to consider the point of view of others are key factors in making the problem bigger or smaller. We want to create growth mindsets that are able to encompass alternative explanations and viewpoints of the problem.

Fixed mindsets are ingrained in *Me* thinking, a person believing that everything is about them. If one believes that everyone is focused on them, watching them, judging them, then they place a great deal of pressure on themselves to be perfect, for every aspect of life to function in a particular way. Having strong empathy and perspective is one of the most essential aspects of a strong growth mindset. As a person gains awareness that other people have needs, hard times, and struggles, just like themselves, they are able to take a step back from situations and consider them from other viewpoints. This often gives them flexibility and lets them relax about making mistakes. If you know no one is perfect and everyone has flaws, then it is not such a big deal when you make a mistake. If you know that everyone has a favorite game to play or subject to research, then you understand that what you want may not always be what is chosen.

Perspective in the Classroom

For some students, just getting to school is an ordeal; getting up and getting to school—even if they are late—represents significant success. Consider also the parental morning experience: before parents of these students get to their own place of work, they have already worked very hard to make sure their child is out of bed, is dressed, has eaten, and gets to school.

Every day we extend perspective-taking, empathy, and understanding into our classrooms. We know that all students need different things. We strive to create an equitable classroom; this doesn't mean we don't support particular students when they need it.

Remind students that perspective and empathy are not about feeling sorry for someone, nor are they about feeling guilty that you have more than someone. Perspective is about understanding other people's lives, needs, and feelings. It is seeing that other people have thoughts and feelings about events, you, and others that can be good feelings or not.

A Practice-Based Learning Environment for Perspective

1. Support students in reflecting on interactions and considering the thoughts and needs of other students.
2. Let students assess situations and make their own *If/Then* statements that will make the problems smaller.
3. Give students opportunities to try again using their *If/Then* strategies to make problems smaller.

Strategies and Activities

Oral Language: Conflict Resolution

1. Discuss with students that there are always two sides to every story so they understand that in every problem involving two people, there can be two different interpretations, two perceived levels of the problem, and two different mindsets.

   We need to be able to explain our side of the story, but we also need to be able to hear the other person explain their problem.

It is always hard to engage in the process of conflict resolution when emotions are high, so it is beneficial to practice the process of conflict resolution around issues and problems we are not personally attached to.

2. Create a simple If/Then as your goal for the problem solving: *If we all listen to each other, then we may be able to make the problem smaller.*
3. Choose a problem that students can relate to, but is not creating problems in their lives at the moment.
4. Pair students with friends they sometimes have conflict with.
5. Instruct students to read out the problem together.
6. Tell students that they can share as themselves; alternatively, they can take on the role of a character from a favorite book or show, or invent a personality. They cannot take the role of another student in the class.
7. Have all students level the problem on the problem scale. See page 16 for more on the problem scale; page 29 for a problem scale template.
8. Discuss their rating of the problem. Did partners agree on the size of the problem? Ask them if it means that one of them is wrong, or if it is possible for two people to level a problem differently?
9. Have each student explain the problem from their point of view. Explain that the most important part is how we listen to another person while they are talking.

10. Remind students what listening looks like. Consider having posters that promote listening on the table while they speak with each other. Ask students what would happen if neither person listens to the other: *If neither person listens to the other, then they will both continue to see the problem from their own point of view.*

11. Ask students what happens when both people listen. In pairs, have them create *If/Then* statements about it: *If both people listen to the other, then they might learn something that they did not know.*

12. Repeat conflict resolution around the same problem; in this case, both friends have growth mindset and are empathetic. Both are open to hearing the other person's perspective; are able to reflect on their behavior and consider what they wish they had done differently; are willing to do something differently next time in order to make the problem smaller

Reading: Read-Aloud and Expand

As teachers, we spend a lot of time searching for great resources to show or read to students. We look high and low for examples or work that will inspire and demonstrate specific expectations that we want to teach. But the most valuable resource of all is at our disposal daily and in abundance: our students' work. The work that students produce is our best resource of all. Have students read their work aloud and use it to drive your lesson.

For Perspective, order the activities so that students use their writing from the Writing activity as read-alouds for the Reading activity.

1. Before the writing period begins, call out the names of three students who will present their work to the class.

2. Assign a writing lesson. You can use the writing activity in this chapter on page 71.

3. During the writing period, check in with students who will be presenting to help them plan what they will present. Encourage them not to write something new, but instead to pick something they have written in a previous lesson. They can spend the writing period proofreading their work and practicing reading it out loud.

Post a chart with the name of each student and rotate through so that every day two to three of your students are reading their writing out loud.

4. When writing period is finished, ask all students but the presenters to clean up. Presenters take their seats in presenters' chairs and decide amongst themselves who will present first, second, and third. If they have remaining time, they can practice their read-aloud a few more times.

5. Have one presenter at a time read their work out loud to their classmates.

> Read-alouds present a great opportunity to reinforce proper listening skills with repeated prompts of the explicit behavior needed while listening:
> - If you were presenting, how would you like your friends to look while listening to you?
> - In order to listen, we need to turn our bodies toward the speaker, shoulders and knees facing the speaker.
> - It is hard to listen and speak, so now is the time to stop talking and listen.

6. When each student is done reading, be ready with group questions that will help students expand their writing together. Using the writing example from the activity on page 71, you could ask:

- Can anyone comment on the detail about the character that helped you get a better sense of the character's strengths or challenges?
- Can anyone list details about the character's strengths that helped you imagine what this character would be like?
- Based on what the author introduced about this character's struggles and challenges, what might be good plot developments?
- This is a great story, with a creative plot. Now the author might want to go back and give more detail about the character in this story. Based on what the author read for us today, what personality traits, strengths, and struggles might they describe at the beginning of the story to set the stage for the problems in the plot?

Writing: Character Development

We can tie everything we are working on with the students into their writing process. We can use writing as a significant tool in our program, covering essential aspects of the curriculum while targeting the social-emotional needs of children. We can have students examine various mindsets and how they influence a character's feelings and actions. Work with students to develop detailed characters by imagining the thoughts and feelings of someone else. Encourage students to infer and wonder about what someone else might think, feel, and do.

1. Go through the books students are reading and photocopy images of characters. Wherever possible, use images that show emotion: images of the character excited, happy, proud, or empathetic; images of the character sad, devastated, angry, confused, upset, or worried.
2. As a class, look at one image together. Take your time detailing a physical description, what the character looks on the outside. Include examination of clothes right down to the patterns on a shirt or dress; not just the color of the hair, but its length and texture.
3. Next, focus on character traits, opinions, and preferences. We can't tell these things from the physical image, but that we can infer and make best guesses to create what the character is like from the inside.
4. Using the Who chart on page 75, record a detailed description of the character, outside (physically) and inside (thoughts and feelings).
5. Once you have practiced with visual images a few times, support the same process without giving students an image. Allow them to create the image of a character in their head.
   - Who is this character?
   - What can you say about them?
6. Prompt students to take risks and develop characters.

In this step, we are asking students to make a guess or create something that is not explicit. Students with fixed mindsets may have more trouble taking a risk and inferring what the character might be like. It can be hard for them to understand that there are no right and wrong answers in this activity.

- Where is the character? Are they standing or sitting? Are they in their room, lying on the bed, talking on the phone, drawing in their sketchbook, reading a book, listening to music?
- What does the character look like? What color is their hair? Is it long and straight? Does it have a slight wave that they try to pin up with a ladybug clip? Did they cut their hair really short because it is easier to take care of?
- What is the character wearing? Does their long flowered skirt cover their ankles? Are they wearing an oversized hockey jersey from their house league team, worn so much the elbows have holes in them?

- How can the character's body tell us what they are feeling? Are they crying into their pillow? Yelling at their mom? Holding their hands over their ears trying to block out the annoying sounds of little brothers?
- What descriptions can you add to the imagery of the character's stance, their body, to show how they are feeling?

Media Studies: Character Problem Scales

In this activity, students work together to create a pamphlet to illustrate different perspectives and ways of thinking about the same problem.

It is often good to have students pick their own images but, for this activity, the image chosen is important, so it is best if you make the choice.

1. Look in books and newspapers for an image of two characters who are in some form of disagreement or struggle. The image needs to capture emotion in the characters' faces and to support students in coming up with different interpretations of the same event. You are looking for an image in which the object or event is small and insignificant, and the characters are dominant. Try to find an image that very closely resembles a repeated problem in the classroom, with enough detail to provoke ideas.
2. Make photocopies of the image. Give each student a copy of the image and the Who: Problem Scale template on page 76.
4. Instruct students to glue the image onto the top box and to take the time to look at the image. Don't let students take their pencils out yet; for the first 10 minutes of the activity, no one is to begin writing. Tell them, "It is thinking and planning time, not writing time."
5. Ask students to consider what is happening in the image. Prompt for connections to confrontations they might have experienced or witnessed:

   Does this remind you of a time that you were playing with your friends?
   Do things like this happen a lot?
   What size problem do you think this is?
   What do you think (describe one of the characters with enough detail for them to know which character you are referring to) is thinking right now?
   What do you think (describe the other character with enough detail for them to know which character you are referring to) is thinking right now?

6. Have students write this description in The Problem section of the Who: Problem Scale. On the first problem scale, students level the problem by drawing a lightning bolt on the place on the line that represents the size of the problem. Students look at the character they have chosen and determine what that character would be thinking inside their head; students will write that in a thinking bubble and place it on the second problem scale.
7. Tell students they can each choose one of the characters from the image and work through the problem scale from that character's point of view.
8. Finally, students draw a new lightning bolt on the last problem scale, showing that the problem stayed at the same level, increased in size, or decreased in size, based on what the character was thinking.
9. Once each student is done, you will have a collection of problem scales that go with one image. They can be gathered to create a pamphlet that explains how different interpretations of the same problem will affect the size of the problem. Students can take this pamphlet home one at a time to show and

explain it to their parents; they can also take it to other classes and read it to students to explain this process to others and build capacity.

> If you have made a few problem scales and created posters from them with students, consider not providing a template for this activity. It is interesting to see where students take it. Some students will struggle with the open-endedness of an activity without clear steps and templates; it is good to include activities that require students to reflect on what you have done before and how they can make the process their own.

Math: Character Survey

In this activity, students create a survey that examines the mindset of a character image.

1. Have students find an image of characters engaged in a challenge or struggle from one of their favorite books.
2. Print or photocopy the image and have them glue it onto the Who: Mindsets sheet from page 77. Students choose one character and describe that character under the image.
3. Have students work up problem scales and thought bubbles for one of the characters. Students write in the first thought bubble the problem from their character's perspective; e.g., *She played with this toy for so long. Then she put it down. It is my turn now.*
4. Ask:

   What would the character think if they thought about the problem from the other student's point of view? Would it be: "Hmm, I guess she was playing with this toy first. Maybe she put it down as part of her game. She probably wants to keep playing with it.

   Students write the new thinking in the second thought bubble.
5. Have students ask classmates to vote on which mindset they believe the characters in the image have and record the votes on the Who: Mindsets chart.

Art/Drama: Two-Sides Collage

In this activity, students create a collage of images from magazines, their own drawings, and photocopies of character images from books.

1. Read aloud a scenario showing someone struggling with a problem. Sample scenarios:

   - You see your friend get their spelling test back. It is full of mistakes. Your friend walks over to their desk and puts their head down.
   - Your friend is reading in front of the class and has a very hard time. They misread most of the words.
   - A student in the class comes in with a new outfit. Their friends make fun of them, saying the outfit is weird.

A problem scale can be used to divide the page.

2. Tell students they will be creating a collage that depicts the two ways of thinking. Suggest that they could place a line down the middle of the page and on one side glue images, draw symbols, and write words that represent thinking that makes the problem bigger; on the other side they can glue images, draw symbols, and write words that represent thinking that makes the problem smaller.

Homework Activities

SAMPLE PERSPECTIVE HOMEWORK ACTIVITIES

Subject	Activity	F	S	S	M	T	W	T
Problem Scale	• Make a problem scale that reflects a conflict you are having with another person; attach a thinking bubble from your perspective and one from the other person's perspective. • Think about a problem you had this week with a friend. Reflect on their point of view. How would they explain the problem? How did they feel during the problem? What were they thinking? What did they go home and tell their parents?							
If/Then	Write an If/Then self-control statement for yourself, based on the other person's perspective.							
Writing	Write an e-mail to your teacher reflecting on a challenge that you have been having at school.							
Drama	While watching TV this week, look at the faces of characters when someone does something nice for them. Look at the faces of the characters when someone does something unkind to them.							
Chores	When you are finished doing a chore at home, examine a parent's face. How do they feel when you help with daily jobs around the house?							

Who

PLACE IMAGE HERE

Physical Description	Character Description

Pembroke Publishers ©2017 *Keep Growing* by Joey Mandel ISBN 978-1-55138-320-0

Who: Problem Scale

PLACE IMAGE HERE

The Problem:

How big a problem do you think this is?

0_____5_____10

Small Problem   Medium Problem   Large Problem

Describe the character you have chosen:

Think about the problem from the character's point of view

0_____5_____10

Small Problem   Medium Problem   Large Problem

The impact the character's point of view has on the size of the problem

0_____5_____10

Small Problem   Medium Problem   Large Problem

Who: Mindsets

PLACE IMAGE HERE

Describe the character you have chosen:

What the character thinks about the problem	How the character thinks about the problem from the other character's point of view
TALLY	TALLY

Pembroke Publishers ©2017 *Keep Growing* by Joey Mandel ISBN 978-1-55138-320-0

7

Initiative

> What it is: The willingness to do something without being asked to or being told what to do. It is the understanding that for each part of the day and each activity, you can wait for others to do the work, or you can participate in the process of looking around on your own, wondering what could and should be done, and doing it and more. It is to anticipate things that need to be done before being asked to do them.
>
> What it looks like:
> - Seeing garbage on the floor and picking it up.
> - Arranging books on the bookshelf without being told to.
> - Working at your desk and adding more detail to your work before telling the teacher that you are done.
> - Noticing that another student is absent and doing their classroom job for them.
> - Being asked to put away your chair and putting away your chair and others that need to be put away too.
> - Problem-solving and using strategies to make a problem smaller.

When the child faces a problem, their ability to initiate a process and follow through with one of their strategies can make the problem smaller. We want to create growth mindsets that allow students to believe that they can solve a challenge themselves because they have the tools to do so.

Students who are willing to engage in an assigned activity use their self-control and mindset to do so. What is the internal motivation that drives students to be willing to stop doing the fun thing and to get down to work? What is it in their mindset that pushes the student to use the self-control to do the hard thing? What is it that students who truly show initiative at each turn of the day have that others do not? What is the thought pattern that lets them delay doing something fun, in order to do something boring first? What pushes them toward an action instead of holding them back?

Each aspect of initiative is about self-control. Initiative is the ability and/or willingness to do something that is not fun or rewarding in itself, but that has some sort of future value. Behind it is a basic understanding or knowledge that the act will hopefully lead to something rewarding in the future.

Initiative in the Classroom

There are many transitions in a classroom. At each transition point, some students push against and challenge the transition, some students move with it but are not helpful, and some students lead the transition. This last group is made up of students who close their books and put them away, who clean up and get ready for what is coming next. We can help students see the role they play in each transition and encourage others to observe and follow. We can encourage all students to set goals for themselves that are one level above what they are working at.

A Practice-Based Learning Environment for Initiative

1. Support students in understanding their role in practice-based learning and their ability to create their own *If/Then* strategies.
2. Help students create *Then*s that recognize the value in doing jobs based in process, not reward, without placing the onus on another.
3. Allow students time to implement *If/Then* strategies without being told to.

Strategies and Activities

Oral Language: Internal and External Motivation

What are some of the internal *If/Then* thinking patterns that students who show initiative use?

1. Ask students to finish these sentences:

   If I put away the chairs, then…
   If I do a good job on my writing, then…
   If I clean up the classroom, then…
   If I see that someone dropped their things and I help them pick them up, then…

2. Examine with the students the type of *Then*s they used to complete the statements. Are they tangible rewards or internal, practice-based rewards? External rewards usually come from someone else in the form of approval, grades, or actual rewards; examples include

   If I put away the chairs, then I might get my name on the Good Helper chart.
   If I clean up the classroom, then I might get extra recess.
   If I practice my piano lesson, then I will get to watch TV.
   If I do a good job on my writing, then my teacher will tell me that I am a fabulous writer.
   If I work a little harder on this writing, then the teacher will tell me I did a great job.
   If I add more detail to this assignment, then my mom will love it.
   If I work harder, then I will get a good mark.

When students work toward internal, practice-based rewards, they are not motivated by a direct reward, to please an adult, or to be praised for actions.

In a practice-based learning environment, develop rubrics in which Level 4 highlights the initiative of the actions, not the final result of the product. Level 4 should highlight doing more than what was asked, adding to something to make it better without direct instruction or reward.

Over time, try to support students to create their own *If/Then* statements involving internal rewards and motivation. We want their completion of actions to be based on their own knowledge that they have done something that makes their work better or does something to help another person.

The action is done for themselves and their own personal satisfaction; examples include

> If I do that section again, then my work will be better.
> If I stop playing right now and clean the room, then I am being fair to my classmates who are following the instructions.
> If I work harder on my writing, then my story will be more interesting.
> If I help my friend clean up her mess, then she will feel good that someone is helping her.
> If I do my classroom chores, then the teacher will not have to ask me over and over to do something that I am supposed to do.
> If I set the table while my dad is cooking, then he will not have to do it himself.

3. In the sharing circle, have students step into the circle if they have done something helpful without being asked.

> *Step into the circle if you have ever set the table without being asked.*
> *Step into the circle if you have ever taken out the garbage without being asked.*
> *Step into the circle if you have ever emptied your backpack without being asked.*
> *Step into the circle if you brush your teeth without being asked.*
> *Step into the circle if you do your homework without being asked.*

4. Explain that what they have shown is called initiative. Ask: *How do you think the person felt when you did something helpful for them without being asked?*
5. Discuss how we show initiative at home.

> *Give examples of things that you do at home without being asked.*
> *Can you think of things to do that are helpful around the house that kids who are a few years older than you do without being asked?*
> *Can you think of things to do that are helpful around the house that kids who are a few years younger than you need to be asked over and over and over to do?*
> *Can you think of things to do that are helpful around the house and that you think would be great to do without being asked?*

If students are not answering or coming up with things, you could give them more direct prompts: for example, *After dinner, when you are done eating, before you leave the table, what might some kids do to show initiative?*
6. Encourage students to self-reflect on initiative: *How many times do you have to be asked to...*
   - *help set the table?*
   - *clean up?*
   - *do your math work?*
   - *come in from recess?*
   - *clear the table?*
   - *participate in group work?*

Have them chart how many times they are asked and the likely result.

SAMPLE INITIATIVE RUBRIC

Level 1	Level 2	Level 3	Level 4
Asked many times then threatened	Asked a few times, then my mom raised her voice.	Asked once and then I did it right away	My mom never asked me. I saw her making dinner, so I set the table.
My mom was mad at me	Frustrated	My mom smiled	My mom stopped what she was doing, came over and hugged me.

7. Have students create negative *If/Then* statements demonstrating the impact of their behavior.

> If my mom has to ask me ten times nicely before yelling at me to come inside for dinner, then she will be disappointed in me.
>
> If my friend has to ask me to help on our group assignment before giving up and doing it on their own, then they may tell the teacher on me.

8. Ask: What *If/Then* statement would help you do it the first time? Brainstorm with students what would motivate them to change their behavior.

Reading: Round-Robin Book Sharing

Sometimes we are so driven by curriculum and assessment in the classroom that we make things bigger than they need to be. We take a small idea or concept and we expand it into a large project to be presented and marked. We explain the success criteria that must be met to receive a good grade and we give students lots of time to work on something. We take the spontaneity and the space for students to engage and be creative out of the assignment. For some students, the time and direct steps help them create a successful project. But for others, the whole process stumps them and they freeze, unable to get any work done. By the time they are ready to present, it is such a huge deal that these students become anxious and do not want to present.

Round-robin presentations can be very effective for some students as they are short and quick; they are over before some students can overthink the task and get stuck. Place the onus on students to present and share books in the classroom that promote a growth mindset and self-control. Instead of presenting information to them, offer them creative ways to take initiative in teaching the information and sharing thoughts and ideas.

Round-robin presentations involve students working in small groups for a short period of time, then switching groups and presenting as the experts in their new group. In the round-robin process, students plan, research, practice, present, and listen.

See pages 118–119 for a list of recommended books that nurture growth mindset.

1. Assign books that cover themes of mindset and self-control, give a book to individual students or a book to each group of two.

Students will not need too much time for steps 2 and 3: depending on their age, students can practice reading the book three times and complete the sheet in one or two periods; then they are ready to present.

Students of varying ages love picture books, even simple ones. The level of difficulty can vary greatly, making them excellent for use with readers of differing abilities.

2. Have students practice reading the book. Use *If/Then* mindset prompts: *If you read the book a few times, then you will notice more things in the book each time you read.*
3. Have students complete a Discussion Ideas sheet; see template on page 88. Instruct them to complete the discussion sheet to help the audience talk about the book. They can write the answers in point form or full sentences.

Writing: Initiative Rubric

> Initiative is a huge step for some children, especially those with a fixed mindset. They may want to take initiative but they get stuck, thinking there is a specific thing to do and way to do it. They need clear guidelines as to what they can do, which steps they can take to make something better. We want students to be able to take initiative and take action without being given precise instructions; we want them to take risks and do things without being told. But this process is too much for some kids. It is up to us to outline steps for them to take and trust that in time, with these guidelines, they will be able to gradually take more risks and show more initiative.

With students, create rubrics that detail the steps that they can take, without you telling them to, so they can move their work from one level to another.

SAMPLE RUBRIC

Level 1	Level 2	Level 3	Level 4
You did not begin your work. You walked around the class making noise. You kept asking the teacher for help. You kept talking to your friends.	You worked quickly and did not complete or review your work. Then you went right to the teacher and said you were done.	You worked slowly, followed the writing process, and reviewed your work on your own. You added something to make it better and made some corrections to your work. You then asked a friend to look over your work. You looked up a few words in the dictionary. You read your work over one more time to see if there were any details you missed.	You worked slowly, followed the writing process, and reviewed your work on your own. You added three things and made many corrections to your work. You asked three other people to look over your work. You asked them for specific feedback and you thought about their ideas. You looked up many words in the dictionary. You read your work over one more time to see if there were any details you missed.
You are missing things.	Add a little more.	Well Done	You Rocked It!

Normally, I am at a level _____. This week, while writing, I will try to work at a level _____.

I will do this by _____

_____

I want to work at level _____

Media Studies: Creating a Newsletter

Involve students in creating newsletters so they are part of the process that goes into sending a message from school to home.

1. Discuss with the class the sections that readers at home would like to see in a newsletter. Have each student contribute, even if each writes as little as one sentence for each, in order to add their voice to the class newsletter.
2. If you have a larger idea or message you want to convey to the parents, brainstorm and plan your message with your students. Assign one or two students the task of putting it into the newsletter. For example, if you would like parents to know the language and goals you have for students for a particular subject or classroom job, co-create a rubric or *If/Then* statements with students to send the information home to the parents.
3. Work with students to brainstorm and chart what a person showing initiative thinks and looks like. Choose classroom routines and ask students the thoughts and actions they have in response to your request to perform them.

   What are you thinking when I say that it is time to clean up the classroom and get ready to go home? What do you do once I have said it?

4. With students, act out scenes of a teacher asking students to perform classroom routines and being ignored, having students seek approval for each action, etc. For example, act a scene in which you ask students to get ready for home and everyone just ignores you and keeps playing; act a scene in which students tell you each thing they put away: "Look, teacher, I am putting away this marker and this pencil."
5. Work up very detailed descriptions of what actions look like at each different level for a rubric chart on the board or interactive whiteboard.

SAMPLE INITIATIVE RUBRIC CHART

	Level 1	Level 2	Level 3	INITIATIVE
Thinks Like	*I should not have to help clean the room. Someone else will do it. I want to keep playing.*	*I wonder what I should do. I will do just a little, then other people can do their share.*	*I can contribute until the classroom is clean. Then I will get my stuff.*	*The more I do, the easier it will be for other people. I can do more and make it better.*

If you have access to only one computer in your class, this activity can be done by the whole class. Introduce the concept to one student at a time during any centre-based activity or as an alternative to silent reading.

Be sure to do this in a positive way. Your tone will influence the effectiveness of this process.

		I will get my own stuff ready.		
Looks Like	You talk with your friends, continue to do what you want, play with your friend in the classroom.	You ask your teacher what you should do, if you should put the chairs away and get your stuff. You tell your teacher that you are going to put the chairs away and list for them the chairs and other things that you put away.	You look around to figure out what needs to be done. You start cleaning the classroom and keep on cleaning until it is done.	You look around to figure out what needs to be done. You start cleaning the classroom and keep cleaning unitil it is done. You find one more part of the room that could use tidying or sorting and you do it quickly, without asking or telling.

6. Brainstorm routines students perform at home. Present them with the Task Rubric and ask them where their actions usually fall. This information can be added directly into the newsletter and will help parents understand the expectations of their children at school.

TASK RUBRIC

Level 1	Level 2	Level 3	Level 4
I do not do the job that I was asked to do.	I wait to be asked to do the job a few times. I do it really fast then say that I am done. I wait for someone to tell me what to do next.	I do exactly what was asked. I look around to see what I can do next.	I do the job I was asked to do really well. I add something more to the job. I look around to see what I can do next.

7. Ask students what they could be thinking to help them do more? This information can be added to an *If/Then* section of the newsletter.

If I vacuum for a little longer, *then* my mom will be really happy.

If I do the job well, *then* I can be proud of myself.

If I do the job for my mom, *then* I am taking a job off of her plate.

If I do a really good job vacuuming, *then* maybe my mom will tell me that I can watch extra TV.

Math: Self-Reflection Surveys

If we want students to write their own *If/Then* statements, then it is important for them to be able to reflect upon which *Then*s will motivate them to begin tasks. Have students create surveys that examine the type of *Then* that would motivate them to do something hard or that they do not want to do.

1. Brainstorm with the class different ways to write the survey. Discuss different *If*s and *Then*s that would be worth finding information about:

   Are we making silly *If/Then*s or would we like to make *If/Then*s that will help us better understand ourselves? Should we ask our friends if this *If/Then* works for them: *If you eat thirty bags of cookies, then you can have ice cream*? Or would it be more interesting to find out if they would be motivated by this *If/Then* statement: *If you do an extra hour of homework every night, then you can watch an extra thirty minutes of TV*?

3. Encourage each student to create their own list of at least ten *If/Then* statements that would work for them, and use the statements to create a survey that each of their classmates will take. Discuss as a class how similar or different their *If/Then* statements are.

Give some examples with tangible rewards, but also discuss practice-based *Then*s with internal rewards.

4. Explain to students that an *If/Then* is of little value if they cannot follow though with the *If*, or if the *Then* is unlikely or impossible. For example, the *If/Then* statement *If I read every night, then my parents will buy me a car* would motivate most students, but would be unlikely to be accepted by any parent. Tell students: "Effective If/Then statements help you improve and work on something that is hard for you, that you would like to get better at."

5. Have students revise and conduct their surveys. Remind them to include their own responses to their *If/Then* statements.

6. Have each student write up a short summary of the data collected in their survey; they can use chart form.

SAMPLE DATA SUMMARY

Would this *If/Then* statement help you?	Yes	No
If I hand in my homework to my teacher, *then* I can earn a dollar.	20	0
If I go to an extra practice a week, *then* I can have extra dessert.	10	10
If I exercise for 5 minutes a day, *then* I will be healthier.	5	15
If I clean up the classroom, *then* I am being fair to my classmates.	10	10
If we work independently during book club and complete work, *then* we can go out 5 minutes early for recess.	16	4

7. Have students analyze the data they collect. Which of their *If/Then* statements was the most likely to motivate other students? Have them consider if this is because the *If* was relatively easy or because the *Then* was very valuable. Which of their *If/Then* statements was the least likely to motivate students? Have them consider if this is because the *If* was too hard or because the *Then* was not valuable.

Art/Drama: Imagining Initiative

It is helpful to get insight into what the students do at home in order to understand what motivates them, as well as to gather a better understanding of the expectations for them at home.

1. Discuss with students tasks they are asked to do at home; e.g., clearing the table.
2. Present *If* actions in response to being asked to perform a task. Have students close their eyes and imagine the look on a parent's face, how they might feel, and what they might say as the *Then*

> If my parent asks me to clear the table and I get up from the table and turn on the TV, then my parent's face would look like… They might feel… They might say to me…
>
> If my parent asks me to clear the table and they have to ask me over and over again, then my parent's face would look like… They might feel… They might say to me…

3. Relate actions to the idea of initiative:

> If your parent asks you to clear the table four times before you get up and clear the table, then how does your parent feel? Are you showing initiative?
>
> If you are eating dinner, and when you are done you get up and clear your plate, then what would your parent's face look like? How would they react to you showing initiative?

4. Have students share their imagined scenarios:
   - Turn to the person closest to you and tell them what happens at your house after a meal.
   - Turn to the person closest to you and tell them about a time you did something without being asked.
   - Turn to the person closest to you and tell them something you could do at home without being asked that would make your parents or someone else at home happy.

Homework

SAMPLE PERSPECTIVE HOMEWORK ACTIVITIES

Subject	Activity	F	S	S	M	T	W	T
Initiative	Come up with new areas of focus for your nightly homework. Reflect on things that are hard for you and that you could work on.							
Problem Scale	Make a problem scale about a job around the house that your parents have to ask you many times to do, something that, if you do it, you know you don't do as well as you could.							
If/Then Strategies	Write an *If/Then* self-control statement to set a goal for yourself to do this chore without being asked.							
Writing	Weekly Letter Home At home, with a helper, you are working on _____							
Spelling	Study for _____							
Math	Do 5 minutes of mental math. Telling the Time *What time do we get up in the morning?* *(We get up at seven o'clock. That means the small hand points to the 7 and the big hand points to the 12.)* *(We get up at seven-thirty. That means the small hand points to the 7 and the big hand points to the 6.)* *(We need to leave in 15 minutes for dance, because we need to leave for dance at six o'clock. What time is it now?)*							
Manual Skills	I am having trouble tying my shoes. *If* I practice tying my shoes every night, *then* I will eventually learn how to do it. It may take me a while, but that is okay.							
Music	I take piano lessons. *If* I practice piano every night, *then* I will learn new songs.							
Chores	I can pick three jobs around the house that my parents are having trouble doing. I could do them without being asked.							
Other								

Discussion Ideas

What do you think this book has to do with *mindset*?

Make notes so that you can participate in a discussion.
What I think this book has to do with *mindset*:

Specific examples from the book I could talk about to illustrate *fixed mindset*.

Specific examples from the book that I could talk about to illustrate *growth mindset*.

Pembroke Publishers ©2017 *Keep Growing* by Joey Mandel ISBN 978-1-55138-320-0

8

Resilience

What it is: The ability to make mistakes and learn from them; the ability to fall down or do poorly at a task and to use that setback to improve performance the next time.

What it looks like:

- Asking the teacher for extra help after getting a bad mark on a test.
- Self-correcting after giving incorrect facts in a presentation.
- After misunderstanding a situation, apologizing and explaining your error.
- Finishing a race even though you are last.
- Getting up to keep trying after falling down while learning something hard.
- Carrying on and finishing your turn after making mistakes while reading in front of the class.

When a child faces a problem and fails to succeed, their response to the setback will influence their next attempt to face that problem and tackle other problems. We want to create growth mindsets in our students: the knowledge that success is not based on perfection and that there will be bumps along the way; the perception of negative feedback, a bad grade, or the incorrect answer as part of the learning process that can be used toward the next attempt.

Resilience in the Classroom

In order for parents to let go of their children a little and allow them to make mistakes, they need to be able to trust us at school. They need to see that we are there to oversee their children, know when they are able to get back up on their own, and work it out. If children need a little support, parents need to trust that we will be ready to step in, have a peer support them, or be there behind them. It is not good for the child for us to successfully act for them, but we must scaffold what the child needs in order to be successful.

A Practice-Based Learning Environment for Resilience

1. Allow students to create their own *If/Then* strategies, even if their statements don't match the ones you would create for them.
2. Allow students to experience the consequences of ineffective *If/Then* strategies and support them in creating more effective ones.

3. Expose students to natural consequences of their actions and be willing to enforce or follow through on the consequences of incomplete *If/Then* strategies.

Strategies and Activities

Oral Language: Four-Square Sharing

On curriculum night, I replicate the first step of this activity with parents. I have paper on some desks but not others and enough pencils available around the room, but not at each desk. This requires adults to get the supplies they need, by using the critical skills required of children every day in school.

1. Each student gets a piece of paper. Depending on the social-emotional skills of the students, I might start off by handing out paper and pencil to each child; other times, I instruct them to get a pencil and paper. This gives them an initial problem-solving task, before the exercise even begins.
2. Instruct students to listen to the instructions and follow along:
   - Fold the paper in half and then fold it in half again. Open the paper. Take a marker and trace over the lines that have been folded. You should have a piece of paper with four rectangles. Use the four sections to draw in.
   - In the top left rectangle, draw a circle the size of a dime in the middle of the space.
   - In the top right rectangle, start at the bottom centre of the rectangle and draw a tree.
   - In the bottom left rectangle, draw or do whatever you want.
   - In the bottom right rectangle, draw a goat.
3. Allow approximately two minutes per square. Try to say nothing apart from the instructions and answer as few questions as possible. If students don't follow your instructions, i.e., do nothing or walk around the room and chat, ignore it.
4. Once students have finished drawing, ask them to hold up their work and show each other what they have done.
5. Have students Pair/Share by turning to the student closest to them. Students share what they are most proud of and what they found challenging.
6. Invite all students to come to the circle to discuss their work.
7. Use prompting questions to determine the purpose of the activity:

   Can anyone think about the point of this activity?
   Do you think this assignment is important?
   Why would I ask you to do this activity?

8. Prompt to examine student thinking:

   What were you thinking when I asked you to do this?
   Were you confused?
   Was it hard for you?
   Were you able to follow all the oral instructions?
   Do you like to draw and do you think you are good at it? Does being able to draw a goat affect how much you like this activity?

9. Prompt to examine student feelings:

Were you proud of your work?

Were you confident that you were doing everything right?

Were you embarrassed that you did not know what to do?

Were you confused that you did not know what to do?

Were you angry by the vagueness of this assignment?

Were you confused by the point of this?

Were you bored by this assignment?

Were you curious to see what we were going to do?

> I share openly with students that I have never been confident in my drawings and have always been a little embarrassed about my lack of ability to draw. Growing up, I could not color within the lines, while my sister and my best friend were talented artists. So an activity like this would be hard for me. It does not play to my strengths. I would feel like I do not have the ability to draw a goat; I would not know where to start. That would mean that this activity might make me feel frustrated and embarrassed.

10. With students, review the concept of mindset. Explain that growth mindsets result in curiosity and openness to explore a vague and ambiguous assignment and allow it to take its course. Explain that fixed mindsets result in frustration at the unknown or a challenge.

11. Connect mindset, and the self-talk that exemplifies it, to emotion: the type of thinking can influence the emotional response. Present as *If/Then* statements:

> If the internal self-talk is *What is the point of this assignment? Am I doing it properly? What will we do with it?*, then I will be nervous about meeting expectations. The emotion that is likely to come from this is anxiety and worry.
>
> If the internal self-talk is *This is a waste of time. Why are we doing this? I can't draw. This is stupid*, then I will feel frustrated. The emotion that is likely to come from this is anger.
>
> If the internal self-talk is *This is too hard. This is so confusing. I don't know what to do. I can't do this*, then I will feel I have failed. The emotion that is likely to come from this is sadness.

Reading: Scavenger Hunt

Students go on an *If/Then* Scavenger Hunt.

1. Use the template on page 99 or have students create their own *If/Then* statements. Cut out sentence strips with matching *If*s and *Then*s. Make sure there are as many strips as students.

2. Hide the strips around your classroom or outside in a contained area. Your goal when hiding them is for all the students to find one, so don't hide them too well.

3. Once a student finds one strip, it is theirs to keep. They should not continue to look for more. Students read their strips first to themselves, then out loud while trying to listen to the strips that others are reading.

4. Students try to match their *If* or *Then* with the sentence strip that makes sense. Once they have found their match, both students can come to a pre-established area of the room to wait for others.

5. Once everyone finds their matching sentence strip, students can read the full *If/Then* out loud as a pair and explain how they knew that their strips matched.

Writing: Plot

Once we have worked on general writing improvement, it is worth going deeper into character development as a basic writing tool. This will improve general writing, but more specifically written and oral character development can teach children social-emotional skills. We can use stories of heroes as examples for children to see perseverance and growth mindsets that allow characters to be the best they can be. When we create characters of our own in our stories, super-heroes or regular children, we can go deep and examine character traits.

Teach students to make stories more interesting by taking one character trait, developing it, and using it to create a plot. What does the character struggle with? The problem or challenge needs to be rooted in that struggle. Use the story line to write stories that highlight strengths and struggles. Outline challenges and mind-sets that would allow a character to push through obstacles.

We can make a story more interesting by ensuring that character drives the plot. Strong, unique characters can be used to create plots that are interesting if we use the character traits to build the story.

Students will build a plot based on character.

1. Use the Character/Problem chart on page 100 with students to brainstorm how they can take the adjectives used to describe characters and use them to make their stories.

SAMPLE CHARACTER/PROBLEM CHART

Character/Who If the character…	Problem/What Then the character…
struggles to be nice to others	hurts someone's feelings
is hilariously funny	does a prank that doesn't go over well
is lethargic	stops trying or working hard during a game
struggles to think about other people	will play only the games that they want to play
is anxious and needs things to be a certain way	gets mad at their friends in the class because they move their things around
is lazy	gives up during a game

is physically impulsive	• pushes a friend off a structure at the playground • moves quickly and fast, so always ends up running into his friends and pushing them
think of themselves first	always wants to go first and have the first pick
is verbally impulsive	keeps interrupting their friend
is jealous	thinks their friend is better than they are at everything

2. Take students on a thinking and feeling journey through their writing, using the theme of taking initiative and going beyond expectations. With students, establish the process: start with a character challenged by a problem; thinking (mindset) can lead to action to make the problem smaller or larger. Students can use the Actions of a Story organizer on page 101 to plan their writing.

3. Provide a Resilience Mindset rubric for students to use to self-assess how they did on the steps for their writing.

Level 1	Level 2	Level 3	Level 4
I was not sure what to do, so I waited at my desk. *I did not understand what to do, so I talked with my friend.* *I don't like writing, so said I needed to use the washroom.*	*I was not sure what to do, so I looked at the example on the board. I didn't really understand it, so I asked the teacher.*	*I was unsure what to do, but I sat down and looked over the sheets on my table. I looked at the board and read over the examples that we did together.* *I tried to write a few things down on my sheet, but I was still not clear if I was doing it right, so I looked at a few of my classmates' sheets to see if their work was similar to mine. Some things were the same, but some kids had some different ideas too. I went back to my desk and used all the examples I saw to do the best work that I could do.*	*I was unsure what to do, but I sat down and looked over the sheets on my table. I looked at the board and read over the examples that we did together.* *I tried to write a few things down on my sheet, but I was still not clear if I was doing it right, so I looked at a few of my classmates' sheets to see if their work was similar to mine. Some things were the same, but some kids had some different ideas too. I went back to my desk and used all the examples I saw to do the best work that I could do.* *I noticed that a few of my friends were*

			not getting any writing done. I asked a few of them if they wanted help. I did not write on their sheets or tell them the answers, but I showed them my work and told them how I got started
You got stuck and then stopped trying.	You were stuck and you tried one thing. It did not work, so you asked for help from the teacher.	You got stuck and then used strategies so that you could keep working.	You got stuck and then used strategies so that you could keep working. Then you helped other students who were stuck too.

Media Studies: Interactive Choices

Work with students to create a presentation on growth mindset that promotes the idea of pushing through something hard by using interactive choices. Speak with a colleague about having your class present to their class. Students will write and present a TV interview in which a reporter interviews someone who struggles and decides to make a plan to improve themselves.

1. Explain to students that their goal is to convey a message to other students and to convince them to set *If/Then* strategies based on what someone else does to change their own behavior.
2. Have students pick an area of focus, something that relates to them and can teach what they have been working on to another class. Students can base their interviews on skills or situations they struggle with or they can choose to use examples that stand for their challenges. For example, if they find reading very hard, but do not want to talk about that in front of the class, they could use swimming as their example; they can write out the whole interview based on how they feel about reading, but using the example of swimming.
3. Have students partner up. Offer each pair the Interview Planning template on page 102 to use as a guide to help them get their ideas together.
4. Partners work together to write a script.

> Interviewer: You are someone who has so many strengths. You are an amazing basketball player and a great skier. Is there anything that is hard for you?
> Interviewee: Yes, there is. I have a very hard time reading. I find it hard to sound words out. All my friends read books that are way thicker than mine.
> Interviewer: Oh, I did not know that. So do you try to avoid reading?
> Interviewee: No, quite the opposite. I want to improve. Reading is something that I want to get better at. I would not be able to do this if I avoided it.

Interviewer: Oh, interesting. What do you do to improve at something that is hard?

5. Allow enough time for the students to practice presenting their interviews.
6. Before an audience comes into your class for the presentations, clear tables or desks to the sides of the room. Move chairs to create an inner and outer circle, with twice as many outer chairs facing inward toward the inner chairs that face outward. Have your class sit on the outer chairs with their presentations. Give each student of the audience class a seat in the inner circle as they come in.
7. Have all presentations take place at once. Allow 3 to 5 minutes for each presentation.
8. Ring a bell or play music to have audience members stand up and move one seat clockwise so they are facing another pair of your students. Have your students repeat the presentation to a new person.

Math: Self-Reflective Questionnaire

When students have finished the Initiative Survey (page 85) and examined the *If/Then* strategies for that survey, they will likely discover they need effective *If/Then* strategies to attempt and to carry through with things they find hard or do not enjoy doing. If they fall down, make mistakes, or fail at challenging activities, it is harder for them to get back up and try again. Help students see that they aren't as likely to give up during fun activities or things that they are good at and that they like to do. We want to encourage students to develop and use the same strategies they use during preferred activities when they struggle or do not succeed in activities that are hard.

Students can create a personal self-reflective questionnaire that examines various activities that they engage in during the day.

1. Have students reflect on their ability to push through something that is hard and to keep going when there are unknowns or when things are hard.
2. Have them reflect on their willingness to try again with something they messed up, made a mistake with, or were not able to do.
3. Present students with the Push Myself and the Get Back Up questionnaires on page 103. Examine the templates with students. Can they think of other ways to gather information about their ability to push through?
4. Students complete questionnaires independently. Ask them to go to their desks and read over the surveys twice. Tell them they need to think of the questionnaires as a whole before they begin filling them in. Have them ask themselves if they, for example, try harder during writing than when doing math. Do they sit down for longer? Do they correct their work more? They should imagine a few different situations before checking off the sections. For example, if a student who likes to run and is good at it falls down while running, would they get back up and keep trying? Would they do the same thing if what they were doing was something they did not like to do and were not as good at?

5. The blank sections are for students to add activities they do at home on their own or with their family. Have them add at least two activities they like and two that they have to do.

Art/Drama: Character Mindset

Pull a character from the real world and, using the character's strengths and struggles, examine what mindset that character would need to accomplish what they did.

1. Model the process using a person who exemplifies resilience:

> Terry Fox is a real-life character who showed resilience.
> This hero truly pushed himself to his limits and did not back down.

2. Have students imagine his journey.

> Close your eyes and imagine that you are Terry Fox. You are running on the side of a hot road. There is no shade. The sun is beating down on your face, on your shoulders, on your back. You look ahead and there is nothing but road in front of you. There is a slight hill, it goes up very very far. You are running on your prosthetic leg. There are cuts on your leg from where your skin chafes against the plastic from the prosthetic. Your leg is sore. It is bleeding. Your plan was to run for another hour today.

3. Discuss with students what kind of thinking would have made Terry Fox stop. Explain that a fixed mindset decreases resilience.

> What are you thinking right now in your head?
> What thought would not help you finish your race?
> What thoughts would make you feel tired, exhausted, defeated?
> What thoughts would have you focusing in on your leg? On feeling the pain of your leg?

Possible answers:

> *I will never finish, so I might as well stop now.*
> *It is not fair that I am sick.*
> *Why am I doing this?*
> *This is too hard.*
> *My leg hurts.*
> *I need to rest.*
> *My friends are at home watching TV, and I want to be too.*

4. Ask: *If you thought those things, then what would you likely do?* Possible answers: *give up, stop running, cry, feel sorry for yourself, yell at someone, lie down on the side of the road, get into the car.*
5. Ask: Do you think Terry Fox ever wanted to stop? Discuss with students the kind of thinking that would have made Terry Fox decide to keep going. Explain that a growth mindset encourages resilience.

What thoughts would help you keep running?
What thoughts would distract you from the pain in your leg?
What thoughts would help you get past the hill?
What thoughts would get you to keep going?

Possible answers:

> *I just need to get over the hill.*
> *I can do this.*
> *I just need to take one step at a time.*
> *It will be so great if I reach my goal today.*
> *I did this yesterday so I can do it again.*

6. Ask: *If you thought in those ways, then what would you likely do?* Possible answers: *keep running, continue, push through.*
7. Students take on character roles. Have each student to create their own *If/Then* statement that describes what they would do if they were Terry Fox.
8. Students turn to the person closest to then and share an *If/Then* statement for their imaginary run that day. What would you tell yourself? Prompt *If/Then* statements:

> If I felt tired, then I would think…
> If I wanted to stop, then I would think…
> If I thought about giving up, then I would think…
> If I thought I could not do it, then I would think…

Possible answers:

> *If I keep running, then I will be proud of myself.*
> *If I get over this hill, then I will be closer to the finish.*
> *If I keep telling myself that I can do it, then I will be able to.*
> *If I distract myself, then I will stop thinking about the pain in my leg.*

Homework

Subject	Activity	F	S	S	M	T	W	T
Problem Scale	Make a problem scale about something you are not able to do.							
If/Then Strategies	Write an *If/Then* self-control statement so that you can work on and practice learning to do the thing you made the problem scale for.							
Spelling	Study for _____							
Writing	Write a story involving a character who faces a challenge and overcomes it; consider that they might not overcome the challenge right away or on the first try.							

Math	Do 5 minutes of mental math.							
	Equality							
	Answer in an equal equation.							
	What is 1 + 1 + 1 equal to? (It is equal to 1 + 2)							
	What is 2 + 2 + 2 equal to? (It is equal to 4 + 2)							
	What is 3 + 3 + 2 equal to? (It is equal to 6 + 2)							
	What is 4 + 4 + 2 equal to? (It is equal to 8 + 2)							
	What is 4 + 5 + 6 equal to? (It is equal to 9 + 6)							
	What is 100 + 4 + 3 equal to? (It is equal to 100 + 7)							
	What is 2000 – 100 – 3 equal to? (It is equal to 1898 – 1)							

If/Then Scavenger Hunt: *Ifs* and *Thens*

If I fall down,	**Then** I will get back up.
If I get a bad mark on a test,	**Then** I will do more homework in that subject area.
If I can't figure out how to work something,	**Then** I can try different ways until I get it to work.
If I do not make a sports team,	**Then** I will practice more and do more exercise of all kinds.
If I make a mistake while reading in front of other people,	**Then** I will keep reading and finish what I started.
If I have a fight with my friend,	**Then** I will try to talk with them to work it out.
If I write an essay that I do not think is very good,	**Then** I will read it over, make corrections, add more detail, and try to change it.
If I am having trouble keeping up with my friends when we run,	**Then** I will try my best and keep running as fast as I can, but know that they may just be faster runners than I am.
If my teacher gets upset with me,	**Then** I can tell myself that it is okay, but that I can try to do something differently tomorrow.
If my team loses a championship game,	**Then** I can think of the best part about playing this season and be happy with that.

Pembroke Publishers ©2017 *Keep Growing* by Joey Mandel ISBN 978-1-55138-320-0

Character/Problem Chart

Character/Who If the character…	Problem/What Then the character…

Pembroke Publishers ©2017 *Keep Growing* by Joey Mandel ISBN 978-1-55138-320-0

Actions of a Story

Who

Problem

Thinking

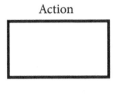
Action

Plot Chart

Who		Develop a character with strengths and challenges.
Problem		Create a problem based on your character's challenges.
Thinking		Show the thinking that will help your character overcome a problem or make a problem smaller.
Action		Show the actions that the character will take to push through something hard or decrease the problem.

Pembroke Publishers ©2017 *Keep Growing* by Joey Mandel ISBN 978-1-55138-320-0

Interview Planning

Describe the character that will be interviewed. List their strengths:
Describe the challenge of the character that will be interviewed:
Interviewer's first question to introduce the character:
Interviewee's answer discussing their strengths:
Interviewer's second question to get information about the character's challenge:
Interviewee's answer that talks about their challenge:
Interviewer's suggestion to give up or avoid problem:
Interviewee's statement that demonstrates their desire not to avoid their problem:
Interviewer's questions about how to make a practice plan:
Interviewee's explanation about their practice plan:
Interviewer's concluding statement:
Interviewee's concluding statement:

Push Myself

Do I push myself when doing these activities?

| | Level 1 | Level 2 | Level 3 | Level 4 | When I find it is hard to do these activities, I tell myself… |
	No	A little	Yes	Absolutely	
In sports					
In reading					
In math					
In a game					
In gym class					
In dance					
In art					
In music					
In					
In					
In					
In					

Get Back Up

If I fall or struggle doing these activities, do I get back up and try again?

| | Level 1 | Level 2 | Level 3 | Level 4 | When I make a mistake or am not able to do something, I am willing to try again the next day when I think… |
	No	A little	Yes	Absolutely	
In sports					
In reading					
In math					
In a game					
In gym class					
In dance					
In art					
In music					
In					
In					
In					
In					

Pembroke Publishers ©2017 *Keep Growing* by Joey Mandel ISBN 978-1-55138-320-0

9

The Home–School Connection

It can be challenging to give parents information and open the doors for feedback. I have found that the more information I send home, the more parents become involved in supporting their children at home. It also helps them let go, as they know I am working my hardest for their children throughout the school day.

How do we, as teachers, build a strong and healthy relationship with the parents of our students? How do we ensure that we are keeping an open communication line with parents, that parents feel they can come to us if they need to and know we will work together? How do we navigate the boundaries between home and school? As teachers, it can seem we want parents to be very involved in all aspects of helping at school, fundraising, field trips, homework, and behavior management. Then it might feel like we set limits that parents are not allowed to cross. While parents might want the school to do all the hard work for them, to solve problems they are not able to solve at home, to communicate nuances and details of each day in explicit and positive summaries, this is not sustainable. Communication from school to home sometimes seems insatiable; the more we open ourselves to communication and sharing, the more a parent's demand for consistent clarification, criticism, and advice grows.

How do we balance these needs? The fact is, teachers have a responsibility to communicate and work with parents. We cannot ask for help in some cases and then not share and work with parents as partners. We cannot give parents suggestions and goals for their children and then not be willing to follow up, listen, problem-solve, and participate in the suggestions they send back to us. And parents can give us useful feedback about things we miss or inform us about another way of doing something. As much as we want to work on the growth mindsets and self-talk of our students, we need to work on these perspectives in ourselves. When a parent gives us feedback, we can use our own growth mindsets to interpret it as professional growth rather than insult.

See chapters 3–8 for homework activities for each character trait; page 36 for information on e-mails home.

Parents need to know the language we use in class. We need to explain growth mindset and self-control to parents, define terms like *If/Then* statements and the *problem scale*. We need to show them ways they can support this learning at home, using curriculum night, newsletters, homework, and e-mails home.

Parent Engagement

Communicate with parents about how they can support their children at home. Parents are unsure as to how to help. Some believe that they should not help their children at all, while others get caught up in making sure their child's homework is perfect and take over the process. Break down for parents the importance of engaging, without doing any of the work for their child.

Curriculum Night

The more frontloading we do as teachers, sharing information in the early fall before the parent–teacher conference, the more we set up the whole year up for success. You can decrease months of unknowns, during which parents get information only from their child and are left confused and frustrated, by helping parents understand the impact of their child's mindset on their learning.

Begin curriculum night by informing parents that you have been working as a class on growth mindset. Share with them the Mindset for Parents reproducible on page 113. Then provide parents with a benchmark chart for general independence milestones in and outside of school; see pages 114–115. Give them a few minutes to read over the information. Ask them to consider the thoughts that went through their heads as they read:

- Were they looking to see where their child was strong?
- Did they notice what their child was not yet able to do?

Encourage parents to share their emotional reaction to the chart:

- Were they nervous when they received the chart?
- Were they happy with where their child was strong?
- Were they sad or upset that their child had not yet hit a milestone?
- Were they angry at the checklist? Did they question its validity?

Explain to parents that the chart is goal-oriented, setting an expectation to be met, recording only if something is achieved or not. How the information on the chart is interpreted and relates to their child is important. Fixed-mindset thinking focuses on what the child is doing and relates it to accomplishment or failure; if interpreted with a fixed mindset, the chart can influence a parent's belief in the success of their children, even in their own success as parents. Make clear that this is not the way the chart should be viewed, that this is not how you view any aspect of their child's day at school, their academics, or their behavior.

Growth-mindset thinking focuses on every child's ability to reach every expectation. If you interpret the chart with a growth mindset, it can be used to help you set daily goals and plans for a child's learning each day. Just as children are at different places in terms of math, language, and physical education, they are at different levels for life skills. As parents and teachers, our job is to be aware of milestones children have yet to achieve and to make a plan for each child for achieving them. This growth mindset interprets the daily challenges of a child as nothing more than the next steps in their learning journey.

Mindset self-talk for parents: "How can I use practice-based learning to set a goal with this chart?"

Parent Questions that Reflect a Fixed Mindset

- What can my child do?
- What can't my child do that they should be doing?
- Is my child advanced or behind?

Parent Questions that Reflect a Growth Mindset

- What can my child do right now? What do they need to learn or practice?
- As parents, what do we do well?
- What could we spend a little more time working on?
- What should we work on right now?
- How will we work on our goals?

Newsletters

Come up with ways that the students can do as much of the work as possible. If you set up a simple format on your computer, students can input important dates to complete upcoming events and curriculum activities.

Use regular newsletters to keep parents up-to-date on classroom expectations and focuses so they can support their children at home. The beauty of a newsletter is that it informs parents about what you are doing in your class. It conveys a clear message to parents of all the ways you are supporting their child each day. The added bonus is that it can help get parents on-board to maintain consistency and to use similar language and messaging at home. Share mindset and self-control information with parents by using explicit and established language. As well as including sections that give a social-emotional focus on sports, funny class moments, reading and writing, and class activities, you can use directed information on mindset and self-control in sections such like these:

Acknowledging Others

Noticing others leads to kinder classrooms. Have students explain what they value, notice, and appreciate about each other, including the *If/Then* strategies they observe each other using.

Mindset

This section explains the social-emotional goal of each newsletter. In it, give explicit details to parents about what you are doing in the classroom to support the trait, as well as explicit strategies that parents can use with their children at home. End with a Mindset Self-Talk statement.

Practice-Based Learning

Practice-based learning offers students opportunities to break down skills and apply them multiple times in multiple settings. It attempts to create environments in which students live out repeated experiences, work on things that are hard, and have the exact tools and strategies to do this. Partnerships with parents are essential to the success of this process. If parents are creating a similar practice-based environment at home, children will be significantly more successful in the classroom. Newsletters are key to transferring this information from school to home. Students learn the information as they consolidate it for their parents, and the information is sent home through the students instead of by the teacher.

Problem Scale and If/Then Self-Control Plan

Always send home examples of classroom challenges that you and your students have solved together using the problem scale. It is a great way to share the language and strategies you are using at school. It also lets parents know about the social challenges occurring in the room and how you are addressing them. For example:

I did not do my homework this week.

0_____5_____10
Not a Problem   Medium-Size Problem   Huge Problem

Provide explicit and detailed *If/Then* statements and strategies you have created with the students, so that parents understand what their child is working on and are able to support the process at home. For example:

I have not been doing my homework very much.

If I continue to not do my homework, **then** it will become a larger problem.

If I _____ ,

(e.g., start doing 5 minutes of homework each night)

then _____ .

(e.g., it will not be a problem anymore and I will improve my writing, which is hard for me right now)

Homework Information and Celebrations

Explain the how the month's homework relates to the character trait of the month. See Homework sections in trait chapters 3–8 for more.

Sample Newsletter Sections: Mindset

Mindset

Mindsets are attitudes and dispositions that influence the way children view obstacles, challenges, and hard situations in life. Fixed mindset is a belief that limits to achievement are predetermined and static. In fixed mindset, the end task or the result is what matters most; a good grade and positive feedback are the measures of success. On the other hand, growth mindset is a belief that intelligence can grow with hard work and effort. It takes into account the value in the process and the learning along the way; low grades might be messages to work harder and feedback is interpreted as ways to improve.

Reflect on your Parenting Mindset

- Is it okay if your children struggle?
- Is it okay if your child fails a test, because they did not study?
- Would you rather your child bring a beautiful project to school because you did most of the work, or that your child hand in an incomplete project because they were not responsible for their homework?
- Would you rather your child never get upset at school because the teacher did not hold your child responsible for their actions, or that your child be held accountable for their actions and receive consequences?
- Would you rather get your child out of trouble at school by arguing your child's side of the story, or allow your child to receive a consequence for their behavior at school?
- If your child complains about another child in the class, do you accept your child's side of the story and give instructions for what your child should say to the other child, or do you encourage your child to reflect on the other side of the story and ask one thing that they wish they had not done?

It is okay to let your child experience obstacles and unknowns. It allows your child experience practicing what to do when there are setbacks.

Parenting Mindset Self-Talk: "It is okay for my child to struggle and face hard moments. It is actually good for them."

Sample Newsletter Section: Responsibility

Responsibility Homework

Homework is not about the final product, it is about the journey of the learning. Homework programs are about *responsibility*. For some students, the very act of bringing the paper to and from school should be seen as homework success. When it comes to the actual work, the process of tackling the homework is more important than the excellence of the result. Teaching your child to do a little bit of homework every night (5 or 10 minutes) creates a process that is manageable and can have a huge impact on areas of schoolwork where they are weak.

Sample Newsletter Section: Independence

Mindset

In school, we are trying to help children gain independence. We hope to help them think first, before turning to someone else with a question that has other people doing the thinking and work for them. You can help your child by stepping back and allowing them to be their own thinker and problem-solver. When they are looking for something, are unsure about something, or ask you to do something for them, help them do it themselves! You can use the following prompts:

- Can you do this yourself?
- What would you do if I was not here?
- Where could it be?
- Let's look around the room and see if we can figure it out.
- How did you do this last time?
- How long did you try on your own first?
- Do you think that there is something you could just try to do first before I help you?
- Yes, I will help you, after I see you working to try to figure it out for two minutes.
- What would you try first?

Consider saying these things to your child:

"I will help you, but I will not do it for you."
"I am not going to do this for you because I know that you could do it for yourself."
"I believe in you. I believe that you have the problem-solving skills to figure this out."
"What is important right now is for you to try to solve this problem yourself."
"Is it better for me to do it for you and for you not to even try, or for you to try to do it, even if you don't get it right?"
"I am not going to do it for you. That would take away your opportunity to try to do it for yourself. It's important for me to give you the chance to try things on your own."
"I can see that this is something that is kind of hard to do the first time. For this one, I am going to show you by doing it first. Then you can have your turn and do it yourself."

For example, when supporting your child on the computer in doing something they can't figure out on their own, take the mouse and show how to do it while explaining what you are doing. Then undo what you did and give your child the mouse. Sit with your child so that they can redo what you showed them. Then celebrate that your child did it on their own!

Mindset Self-talk: "When something is hard, I can try a few things on my own before asking for help."

Independence Homework

- Have your child take out their homework from their bag.
- Help your child find a good location in your home to post their homework checklist; have them check in with it everyday.
- Help your child set goals before the week starts; i.e., highlight the boxes to indicate which activities they plan to do over the week.
- Give your child the job of checking off the boxes and following up.

Sample Newsletter Sections: Self-Regulation

Mindset

Self-regulation is a controlled energy level that is "just right" for the body and mind to be ready to learn. This means that your child is not overstimulated, which makes them too excited, overwhelmed, jumpy, or charged to sit and process learning. It also means that a child is not understimulated, which makes them too sluggish, tired, or distant to learn. When a child's body is calm yet alert, the child is at an energy level that will allow for learning.

If your child is visibly excited, hyper, running around, and not in full control of themselves, discuss with them their energy level and the steps they can take to change it.

- Was it nice to be running around so much?
- Was it fun?
- Did you feel that you were in complete control of your body?
- Is there a difference between running around outside while playing a game and running around at dinner and not sitting down to eat?
- Are there times that it would be nice to be able to slow your body down?
- How could we do that?
- What things can we do that will slow our bodies down?

Each day, help support your child's self-regulation by explaining to them the choices they can make about moving from an exciting and active activity to a slower and calmer one.

Create *If/Then* plans together that work for you and your child; for example:

- **If** I am very hyper after I play tag outside, **then** I could go inside and have a snack to slow my body down.
- **If** I think I am not in control of my body after I play soccer, **then** I could read a book until my energy level goes down.
- **If** I am upset with someone, **then** I could lie down on my back on the carpet and look at old baby pictures of me to change my mood.

Mindset Self-Talk: "When my body feels out of control, there are things I can do to change the way my body moves."

Practice-Based Learning: Waiting

Our children don't get much practice in waiting for something they want or need. When a child is hungry, we go through a drive-through before we get home. When a child feels a little thirsty, we hand them their water bottle. Children do not have to wait for their favorite TV show to come on once a week; they go to Netflix or the DVR and cue up any show they want at any time. Long car rides are fun, because they watch movies or play on electronic devices. While waiting for a sibling to finish an activity, they watch a movie on a tablet. Though each of these events in isolation seems harmless, put together they show a pattern of eliminating the need to learn and practice waiting. Children need to learn to occupy themselves so that they are not bored while waiting, so that they are not running around without control.

Allow your children to wait. Allow them to say "I am bored" and do not rush to find them something to do. Allow them to complain and encourage them to take a positive step to make their situation better. Be willing to model this behavior the next time you are in line, annoyed and frustrated that there is only one cashier. Instead of complaining and wishing that another cashier would come out, consider saying, "Hmm. This might take a while. I noticed that I was starting to feel frustrated by this line. My heart was starting to beat fast. Instead of getting upset about this line, I wonder what I could do to make the time in the line more fun. We could play rock–paper–scissors, we could do some mental math, or we could make up a story together."

Self-Regulation Homework

For more activities, refer to *Moment to Moment: A positive approach to managing classroom behavior* (Mandel, 2013). Self-regulation activities can be photocopied and sent home.

There are some great activities that can help children practice slowing down their bodies. Accuracy sports, board games, sewing, painting, obstacle courses, start-and-stop relay races, and balance activities are all great games that support self-regulation.

Sample Newsletter Section: Perspective

Perspective Homework: E-mails from home to school

If your child comes home upset, please send me a polite e-mail explaining the events from your child's perspective and outlining the facts for me. Try not to add judgment or assumptions about my actions or those of other students, as doing so can lead to defensive e-mails and hurt feelings. Please simply tell the events from your child's perspective and I will be happy to read your e-mail. It is possible that I completely missed the event. Or I may have had a different perspective on the events. If we communicate politely together, we can figure it out. Please have your child sit beside you as you write the e-mail. Better yet, encourage your child to write it.

See page 116 for Perspective E-mail Sentence Wall.

You can use the attached Sentence Wall to support your child in writing polite e-mails that explain the problem from their point of view and consider the problem from the other person's point of view.

Mindset Self-Talk: "There are always two sides to every story. I can try to consider the other side."

Sample Newsletter Section: Initiative

Mindset

Initiative is very hard to teach. How do we teach children to do something without having to tell them to! I find that rubrics help. We can use them to specifically outline the skills it takes to be able to notice what needs to be done and to do it without being asked.

Mindset Self-Talk: "It is better to do things without being asked."

INITIATIVE RUBRIC

Level 1	Level 2	Level 3	Level 4
I did not do what I was asked to do.	After being asked a few times, I sort of did what was asked of me.	I did what I was asked to do.	Without being asked, I noticed what is usually done for this activity or for this chore and I did it.

Initiative Homework

PRACTICE-BASED INITIATIVE HOMEWORK RUBRIC

Level 1	Level 2	Level 3	Level 4
My parents told me to do my homework many times and I did not do it. • I said I would, then did not. • I started arguing with them. • I yelled at them. • I walked away.	After being asked to do my homework a few times, I sat down and did some of it quickly, but not very well.	When I was asked to do my homework, I did it.	I looked at my checklist and decided what I would work on by myself. I started with what I needed to do tonight. Then I picked one more thing to work on. I set up my homework and completed it on my own. I looked it over one time to try to make it better.

Sample Newsletter Sections: Resilience

Mindset

Resilience is the ability to continue to work at something when it is hard, to not give up, walk away, or melt down when something becomes confusing or difficult. It is also the ability to start again another time or another day after making a mistake, falling down, or failing. When your child is resilient, they are able to move through the hard moments, finish a task, and ultimately realize that it was not impossible. These experiences build on each other and make your child more willing to begin another hard task and accomplish it.

It's hard to be willing to let your child fall down, make errors, or fail. Your instinct as a parent is to rush in to save, protect, and defend your child. But if you do this each time they forget something, make a poor choice, or make a mistake, then you are depriving them of the chance to experience setbacks and hard moments. By fixing your child's mistakes, you send a message to them that errors should not happen and must be solved by someone else, instead of letting them experience the mistake and learn from it. If you bring to school what they have forgotten at home, you are taking away the experience that will motivate them to try harder next time. If you defend them in peer conflict without asking them to consider the other sides of the story or their role in the conflict, you are reinforcing their one-sided interpretation.

Parenting Mindset Self-Talk: " I can let my child fall. I can let my child experience unknowns and missteps. Schools are there to help my child through these hard moments in a safe and caring environment. I can take a step back and let my child experience life's adversities."

Practice-Based Learning

Math: Identify an area of math that your child finds hard. Teach them how to work on something that is hard. Go back to the basics. Return to a similar concept that is much easier. Practice it each day by working on the same kind of problem for 5 minutes, gradually increasing the level of difficulty.

Sports: If you are playing a sport against your child, play one small level above them. Do not play below them, each time, so that they win each game. Do not play at your level, beating them every time and monopolizing the game. Instead, make opportunities for them to face setback and keep playing. Play the sport to teach them.

Board Games: As a parent, be willing to win when you play games with your children. Let them practice losing with you there to help them monitor and reflect on their reaction.

Mindset Self-Talk: " I can face something that is hard by working on it."

Mindset for Parents

Mindsets are attitudes and dispositions that influence the way children view obstacles, challenges, and hard situations in life.

A *fixed mindset* is the belief that IQ is predetermined and static. In fixed mindset, the end task or the result is what matters most. The product at the end is how the task will be judged. A good grade and positive feedback are the measures of success.

On the other hand, a *growth mindset* is the belief that intelligence can grow with hard work and effort. People with growth mindsets understand the value in the process and the learning along the way. Low grades might be messages to work harder; feedback is interpreted as giving ways to improve.

Research shows that, regardless of standard measures of intelligence, individuals with growth mindset do better on tests, on hard tasks, and in personal aspects of life. We can help build growth mindset. We can create environments that support your child in valuing and developing the work they put into accomplishing something, rather than focusing our celebrations on the successful end product. For example, encourage and praise your child while they practice kicking the soccer ball and doing drills, instead of cheering only when they score a goal.

We help children build a growth mindset by creating an environment with the core belief that children can learn any skill if we break it down into small enough chunks for them and put time and energy into helping them practice that skill. Practicing anything at their level, and practicing it over and over and over, will help a child improve in any aspect of life, even and most specifically aspects that are very hard. This is called *practice-based learning*. It is based on the belief that if we are taught properly and taught well, if we are taught all the hard skills that go along with learning something difficult, then we can learn it.

One of the most important strategies of practice-based learning is *self-talk*. While we break down a skill for a child and teach them how to read, do equations, self-calm, or skip rope, we can talk out loud in positive, problem-solving, and process ways. For example, we can say, "Hmm, I have not skipped for awhile, I wonder if I can do it. Well, I will only know if I try. Let me see, I will need to make sure that I get the rope over my head, so I will have to move my arms up high. Oops, no. That did not work. That's okay. I will try it again. No, that one hurt. How can I try this differently so that I can make it work?" Modelling self-talk aloud will help your child think through problems in a positive way themselves and understand the process of meeting a challenge.

Pembroke Publishers ©2017 *Keep Growing* by Joey Mandel ISBN 978-1-55138-320-0

General Independence Goals for Children at Home and at School

Grade	Morning Routine	School	Homework	Chores	Problem-Solving
JK	Can • get dressed on their own. • put waffles in the toaster and push down. • get their own cups if low enough to reach. • fill cups up with water from the tap. • get up and go pee on their own.	Can sit during a 10-minute carpet lesson.	The homework system relies on parents. Materials brought from home to school are done completely by adults.	When asked and when someone is with them, will attempt to put some of their toys away in bins or areas of the room.	If eating cereal and need a spoon, will call out that they need a spoon. If told that they can go get something, can go and find it on their own, if it is in an accessible area in the house.
SK	Able to put all their clothes on by themselves.	Can work at a play-based center for 10 minutes with other students.	When told at school to do something really important when they are at home, can transfer that information, possibly with a prompt: "Do you have something important to tell me?"	When someone is with them, cleans up after an activity.	When opening something that is hard to open, they can get scissors on their own and open it.
1	Can • brush their teeth on their own, but with supervision. • carry their own backpack to and from school. • dress themselves, including outdoor clothing (e.g., pants, coats, velcro shoes.)	With explicit step-by-step instructions, can sit in a group and work without a teacher on a simple activity that that is similar to something that they have done before.	Can • bring something from home to school with reminders both at home and at school. • bring material home to complete a task that takes about 10 minutes. • with prompts from the teacher, take homework out of their bag and give it to the teacher (including setting up at table).	Can help do family chores: e.g., set table with support, yard work with an adult.	If their jacket zipper is stuck, they can pull at the zipper and try to get it unstuck.

Pembroke Publishers ©2017 *Keep Growing* by Joey Mandel ISBN 978-1-55138-320-0

General Independence Goals for Children at Home and at School (continued)

Grade	Morning Routine	School	Homework	Chores	Problem-Solving
2	Learning to tie shoe laces. Can pour their own cereal.	Can • sit at a desk for 20 minutes and look and listen to someone talking. • work to try to figure out what they are missing when given partial instructions.	Can • bring home to complete material that takes about 10 minutes. • set themselves up at a table and complete the work.	Can do family chores on their own. When asked, will set the table by themselves. Can clear the table by themselves.	If stuck or can't solve a problem, will ask for help, but when told to try to figure it out on their own, are able to look around and try to solve the problem.
3	Can • put toast in the toaster. * spread cream cheese or peanut butter on toast.	Can sit at desk for more than 30 minutes and listen to a lesson.	Can put homework in a special bag or duo-tang and bring it back to school.	With a checklist, can do family chores independently: e.g., vacuum, sweep. Will do more detailed personal chores, like put their own laundry away.	Can realize that their device needs batteries and can find and change the batteries on their own.
4	Can • make their own breakfast. • get their materials for school and put them in their backpack. • make their own bed.	Can get out agenda and fill in homework and important dates independently.	Can do homework for a few different classes in one night and work for up to 30 minutes.	Can independently do detailed family chores: e.g., clean up and do the dishes after dinner; fold and put away laundry.	If they forget something important at school, they find a way to complete the task; e.g., making something again or using something different.
5	Can help make their own lunch in the morning.	Can work for more than 30 minutes independently of the teacher on a group project with set roles.	Can bring home their work from school and edit it; i.e., read it over and make it better, using checklists and rubrics.	Can help for more than an hour with a large family clean-up or chore.	Can try to fix an electronic device or a bike on their own, before asking for help.
6	Can • do a few family morning chores. • take out the garbage on garbage day. • remember the different materials needed for different days of the week; e.g., "On Thursday, I need my piano books for after-school lessons."	Can sit for an hour and • write an important test • work on an important assignment independently.	Can bring a multi-step project home and complete it independently using a checklist.	Can help with a hard or unpleasant chore until it is done; e.g., cleaning something unpleasant (wash-room) or fixing something that is complicated.	Can look for something misplaced they need for school in multiple places before asking for help.

Pembroke Publishers ©2017 *Keep Growing* by Joey Mandel ISBN 978-1-55138-320-0

Perspective E-Mail Sentence Wall

Salutation

Dear _____
    Teacher

Positive Intro

I hope you are well.
I can't wait to see you.
Did you have a nice day?

My favorite part of the day was when I/we _____.
                    read _____
                          stories
                          during silent reading
                          a book outside
                    sang songs
                    wrote a story
                    played _____
                          football
                          soccer
                          tag
                    learned something new
                    ate an amazing _____

I _____ it because _____.
   loved   it was something I have never done before
   liked   we all got along
   appreciated   it was exciting
   enjoyed   it was new
                        it was relaxing

Body of the Message

I had a _____ day at school today because I _____.
        hard   got hurt when _____
        sad   felt nervous when _____
        tricky   did not understand _____
        miserable   was left out of _____
        challenging   could not figure out how to _____
        difficult   got in trouble for _____
                          had a fight with _____
                          was hurt by _____

I felt _____ because _____.
      mad   you did not let me _____
      sad   someone told me to _____
      jealous   let other kids _____
      embarrassed   said that _____
      nervous   made me _____

Pembroke Publishers ©2017 *Keep Growing* by Joey Mandel ISBN 978-1-55138-320-0

Final Thoughts

I had been thinking about writing this book for a while. My final push came when I was watching the news, a story about the Santa Claus parade. The organizer said that the year's parade was going to be bigger and better than ever: there were more floats and they were much bigger; there were more bands and greater sights to see. As I heard this, a fear went through me, a fear for my children, for the students I teach, and for me as a person. How can we ever be happy at home when we open Facebook for a minute and read about all the incredible things our friends are doing or in our classroom learning from a blackboard without fancy lights flashing? How can we be content if each year, each movie, every playdate, and any workshop that children encounter needs to be brighter, flashier, and cooler than before? What is left? If each cake they eat is more delicious, if each present they get is bigger, will it ever be enough? Can we ever be satisfied? If the next video game looks so real that it appears that they are actually in it, how can my students ever be interested or focused on my math lesson, given on a whiteboard with boring little me explaining something to them?

We keep telling students that the process is what is important, but their lives are full of end products. Their lives are about the perfection of the final product and they demand more and more from everything. When the Santa Claus parade is spectacular, when their classmates are on select competitive sports teams, when projects done at home come to school and wow the teacher, there is enormous pressure to create and produce things of perfection. It must be hard to be a learner in that process, to take chances and participate in activities that need work to be mastered. Venturing into the unknown and the unclear might seem overwhelming, as the value of the final product and one's accomplishment is so clear in comparison.

Children with growth mindsets are able to take more risks and attempt the unknown, because they know that the learning takes place in the process. We can't simply explain that concept to students; we have to create teaching environments that support it. The real work that needs to be celebrated is the conversation between two students through which they hear each other's voices and compromise together; a child going off on their own, taking a bunch of pucks, and working on their shot, even if they miss almost every one of them; or a student who struggles to read chooses books at their level sitting down with them and trying to sound out words on their own. The moments that show a willingness to practice and work at something hard are the moments to notice and acknowledge.

Every day we need to remember that it is the process that we are teaching. Children will fail, make mistakes, and forget things, and it will be frustrating for parents and teachers who are trying to move forward. But our reactions to those moments and our goals at the time need to be thought out. They need to allow each student to be aware that a mistake occurred and to care about it enough to take one active step, one positive movement forward. They need to prepare the student to do something different the next time in an attempt to not make the same mistake again. That is success, that is real growth.

Recommended Books on Mindset

Here are a few summaries of mindset books. When you have a few extra minutes take the time to read these treasures to your students. I typically read them near the end of the year, after we have done a lot of work on mindset and self-control. I tend not to do big activities around these books; I just read them to the students and have them share their thoughts with me. I tend not to begin the discussion by prompting students with words like *mindset* or *self-control*, but I find that the students are able to make the connections.

Happiness Doesn't Come from Headstands *by Tamara Levitt*

This book is about a girl who can't do a headstand. All of her friends can do them, but she can't. She practices, she works at it, she spends all her time trying, her friends help her, yet she just can't do it. Then she finds joy in other things. She continues to work on the headstands, but realizes that she can do other things and that she can be happy about.

This book depicts mindset, initiative, and resilience as it begins with a child who is unwilling to give up even though she can't do something that all her friends can. She works and works and takes on her challenge with determination. What makes the message very strong is that, at the end of the book, she does not learn how to do the headstands (yet? maybe? Who cares?). The book does not end with the typical message that hard work pays off with full reward, because sometimes it does not. But she finds happiness elsewhere. She works at her goal and then changes it.

The Girl Who Never Made Mistakes *by Mark Pett and Gary Rubinstein*

This book is about nine-year-old Beatrice, who has never made a mistake. She never forgets her homework, wears mismatched socks, or drops things at talent shows. The book shows images of Beatrice going through daily activities with strangers or her fans following her because she is the girl who never makes mistakes. Beatrice opts out of activities with her friends because she might make a mistake. Finally, on stage, in front of everyone, she makes a mistake. With all eyes on her, she laughs. She faces a mistake and she moves on from it. From that point on, she is able to have more fun, be silly, and play with her friends. At this point in the book, there are no longer people watching her. The pressure of those watching her has gone away.

Children with fixed mindsets believe that mistakes show they are not smart or capable. Therefore, they put immense pressure on themselves not to make mistakes. Over time, they begin to believe that others put the same pressure on them, that others are watching them, impressed by their successes but disappointed in their failures. Some people with fixed mindsets live their life as if they're performing or being watched by others, that the world is watching them. They think that people are judging them and that they need to do things perfectly all the time. This affects their willingness to take risks, try hard things, and made mistakes.

This book beautifully illustrates the idea of other people watching with an expectation of perfection. The fixed-mindset child struggles to take risks because of the fear of what others will think about them.

The Empty Pot by Demi

This book is about an emperor looking for a successor. The emperor gives all the children in the village a seed to grow and tells them to come back in six months. The child who can grow the best seed will be the next king. The story follows Jun, who is a talented gardener. But over the six months, despite all his efforts, his plant does not grow. After six months, all the children return to show their creations. All the children bring stunningly beautiful plants, but Yun's pot is empty. Embarrassed, Yun bows his head and walks forward holding his pot. The emperor declares him the next king, as he is the only child honest enough to admit that he was unable to grow anything. The seeds had all been boiled and no plant could have grown from them.

Children with growth mindsets are able to handle challenges. As the seed refuses to grow, Yun is shown working away at his problem. He attempts many different things, working independently and consistently in order to try to fix something that is not working. Finally, when it is time to show what he has, this child is able to admit that what he has done did not work. He does not make up success to impress others.

The Dot by Peter H. Reynolds

This book is about a young child who does not like art class. The child sits in art class, stuck and unable to create anything. When the child complains to the teacher, the teacher tells the child to just do something. The child smashes a dot on the page. The teacher tells the child to sign it. The child does. The next day the child is surprised to see their art work, framed and displayed in the classroom. Over time, the child continues to do more dots and add things to the dots. The child goes on to help others succeed in creating their own art.

The first page shows the behavioral result of fixed mindset. Stumped by something hard, the child is unable to produce anything. If a child has a fixed mindset, believing that they can't make mistakes and need to produce brilliant work, then it can be very hard to begin work and try to do something that does not come naturally. The teacher is able to support the child to begin work, not by helping the child create an amazing work of art, but by seeing success in something smaller. Then each day, the child is able to take risks and add to and improve what they started.

Acknowledgments

Thanks to my great friends Lisa Byrne, Laura Cornish, Ginnelle Elliott, Hannah Sung, Kirsten Osterback, Shannon Greene, Velvet Lacasse, and Jill Sanderson, who each went above and beyond to help me with this book and inspire me every day. Thank you to the supportive staff at Pembroke Publishers. Finally, my gratitude to my husband Mike Mandel, who helps me keep growing and cares for me deeply.

Resources

Recommended Books for a Growth Mindset

Picture Books

Extra Yarn by Mac Barnett
A Spot Of Blue by Elaheh Bos
The Tiger in My Chest by Elaheh Bos
Voices in the Park by Anthony Browne
My Mouth is a Volcano! by Julia Cook
Personal Space Camp by Julia Cook
Thanks For Your Feedback, I Think by Julia Cook
The Day the Crayons Quit by Drew Daywalt
What Is A Thought? by Amy Kahofer and Jack Pransky
Thinking About Thoughts by Leanne Matlow
The Most Magnificent Thing by Ashley Spires
Whole Body Listening Larry at School by Kristen Wilson & Elizabeth Sautter
What Do You Do With an Idea? by Kobi Yamada

Books for Novel Study

The One and Only Ivan by Katherine Applegate
Because of Mr. Terupt by Rob Buyea
Out of My Mind by Sharon M. Draper
Looking for X by Deborah Ellis
Wonder by R.J. Palacio
The Book Thief by Markus Zusak

Professional Resources

Chissick, Michael and Sarah Peacock (2013) *Ladybird's Remarkable Relaxation.* London and Philadelphia: Jessica Kingsley Publishers.
Crooke, Pamela and Michelle Garcia Winner (2011) *Social Fortune or Social Fate.* San Jose, CA: Social Thinking Publishing.
Dweck, Carol (2006) *Mindset: The New Psychology of Success.* New York, NY: Random House.
E-Learning, http://visuals.autism.net/main.php?g2_item

Huebner, Dawn (2006) *What to Do When You Grumble Too Much: A Kid's Guide to Overcoming Negativity, What to Do Guides for Kids*. Washington, DC: Magination Press.

Huebner, Dawn (2007) *What to Do When Your Temper Flares: A Kid's Guide to Overcoming Problems With Anger, What to Do Guides for Kids*. Washington, DC: Magination Press.

Johnston, Peter H. (2012) *Opening Minds: Using Language to Change Lives*. Portland, ME: Stenhouse Publishers.

Kuypers, Leah (2011) *Zones of Regulation*. San Jose, CA: Social Thinking Publishing.

Mandel, Joey (2014) *Anxiety: Deal with it before it ties you up in knots*. Toronto, ON: James Lorimer & Co.

Mandel, Joey (2013) *Moment to Moment: A Positive Approach to Managing Classroom Behavior*. Markham, ON: Pembroke.

Mandel, Joey (2014) *Stop the Stress in Schools: Mental Health Strategies Teachers Can Use to Build a Kinder Gentler Classroom*. Markham, ON: Pembroke.

Mischel, Walter (2014) *The Marshmallow Test: Mastering Self-Control*. New York, NY: Little, Brown and Company

O'Neill, Catherine (2008) *Relax*. Swindon, UK: Child's Play.

Shea, Donna and Nadine Briggs (2015) *I Feel Mad! Tips for Kids on Managing Angry Feelings: How to Make & Keep Friends Workbooks, Volume 1*. Boxborough, MA: How To Make And Keep Friends LLC.

Shanker, Stuart (2013) *Calm, Alert, and Learning: Classroom Strategies for Self-Regulation*. Toronto, ON: Pearson.

Thich Nhat Hanh (2008) *Mindful Moments: Ten Exercises for Well-being*. Berkeley, CA: Parallax Press.

Wagner, Aureen (2000) *Up and Down The Worry Hill*. Rochester, NY: A Lighthouse Press Book.

Winner, G. Michelle (2007) *Social Behavior Mapping: Connecting Behavior, Emotions and Consequences Across the Day*. San Jose, CA: Social Thinking Publishing.

Winner, G. Michelle (2007) *Thinking about YOU Thinking about ME*, 2nd edition. San Jose, CA: Social Thinking Publishing.

William, Mary Sue and Sherry Shellenberger (1996) *How Does Your Engine Run? The Alert Program for Self-Regulation*. Albuquerque, NM: Therapy Works Inc.

Index